Jo
___

Members of Jim Driver's *Writers' VIP Club* get free books, articles and videos about writing and self-publishing. They are always the first to hear about new books and events.

See the back of this book for details on how you can sign up for free.

OUTLINE YOUR BOOKS
OR DIE

Secrets of Writing Fiction that Sells, including Plotting and
Novel Outlining Techniques

JIM DRIVER

Third Edition | April 2020

Before We Get Started

Introduction

IT'S PRACTICALLY impossible to write a bestselling novel unless you work from some kind of outline. Just ask successful authors such as James Patterson, JK Rowling, and Stephen King.

At this point, fans of Stephen King are going to be screaming that I'm wrong, that he pours scorn on the very idea of outlining. Maybe that's what he says, but in *On Writing*, King instructs fledgling authors to put their efforts into creating a 'spontaneous' first draft. To my mind, that's nothing less than a labour-intensive way of outlining.

The only hugely successful author I've come across who never outlines is Lee Child. His method of writing is to construct a novel scene by scene. It's a laborious process but he writes slowly (500-1,000 words a day) and concocts his novels in one draft. Even so, I genuinely do have the feeling he has more of an idea of what's going to happen than he lets on.

The method I'm going to show you is less time-consuming and more user-friendly than either of those utilised by the two giants of contemporary story-telling. Once you get used to the process, it shouldn't take you more than a few hours to produce a workable outline for a novel or screenplay in any genre.

Story gurus such as Robert McKee, Syd Field, and John Truby have almost turned storytelling into a branch of science. They compile charts dotted with mysterious phrases like *Character Arc, Point of No Return, Rising Action,* and what-have-you. People pay thousands to go on weekend seminars to unravel the mysteries of storytelling. There are even three- and five-year university courses studying nothing else.

Don't get me wrong: I think it's good that writers know about the Three Act Structure and the nuts and bolts of story-telling. I've even put together a book that explains all that stuff. It's called *How To Write The Million Dollar Story.* If you think it might help you, feel free to check it out.

There are hundreds of books out there claiming to show the 'secrets of outlining'. Problem is, they almost all suck. I know, because I've read almost all of them.

The majority rehash tired old ways of stringing together Plot Points, Inciting Incidents, and so on, to create a pile of index cards saying stuff like, *John sells Bleak House to Jane, but unbeknown to him, she was the one who instigated the infestation of rats.*

You'll already have worked out that the title of this book is a slight exaggeration. You will not *literally* die if you decide not to outline, but it could seriously damage your career as a bestselling author. I've written novels and short stories every which way, and I can tell you that my method of outlining is the easiest and best I've come across. I also keep refining it, which makes it better and better.

Note about Language: Being from the UK, I'm writing in British English and so readers in the United States may notice some deviation from the spellings you are used to. For example, instead of 'realized' it's *realised,* people wear trousers because pants are what they wear *under* their trousers, and so on. I hope this deviation will not spoil your reading enjoyment too much.

My Search for the Ultimate Outline

I've been outlining fiction for many years. In my time, I've ghostwritten a total of 22 works of fictions under various pseudonyms and guises. From time to time, I've also been paid to compile outlines for other authors, who've gone on to use them to write their own novels. You could say, I've been there, done it and got the T-shirt.

When I first started, I used the methods taught by leading gurus, and it would take me quite a while to construct a fairly straightforward outline.

A little while ago, I decided to create a new detective series and publish it under my own name. I wanted it to be something I could be proud of. The characters excited me, and I'd worked out a vague three novel story arc that I thought would work well. All I needed was to outline the individual novels and make sure it all worked together as a trilogy.

I soon realised the techniques I'd been using up to then just weren't up to the job. It took me ages to construct an outline, and I was getting clunky results. The old, traditional methods of outlining just weren't doing it for me.

I tried and I tried, but I could never any further than plotting the first 38 chapters of the first volume. [As I'd decided to write short, snappy chapters, this would be less than a third of the projected novel.]

All right, I knew roughly how each book was going to end — which meant I also knew how the next one one going to begin — but outlining the individual chapters was complicated by the timelines and by the number of characters involved.

I decided to get stuck in and wrote the first 45,000 words from what I'd already plotted, hoping that would spark me into action, but it didn't. The characters didn't talk to me, and the plot was all over the place.

I knew I needed a find a better way of outlining, so I decided to spend time (and money) on research. My first call was to an online Masterclass conducted by the world's best-selling thriller author, James Patterson. These days, he writes almost exclusively with co-authors, so I suspected he'd be big on outlining. And he is.

I'd read a couple of James' early novels. I liked his short, snappy chapters, and I was fascinated by the number of surprising twists and turns he managed to build into each plot. During the masterclass, James came across as a nice guy, and he seemed open and revealing about the way he works.

What I learned was useful, and inspiring, but it still wasn't enough. Afterward, I visited a bookshop and picked up an armful of his novels. To be honest, I was disappointed by what I read. Although his stories are well-crafted and genuine page-turners, his characters and his writing style just don't do it for me.

A while later, I realised why I felt like I did. Running over what he'd said in his Masterclass, I found out James Patterson was writing with a particular reader in mind (and that reader wasn't a late middle-aged writer from England). I learned a lot from that one revelation and I'll talk more about it later.

After taking the James Patterson Masterclass, I bought just about every book about plotting and outlining I could lay my hands on. Practically all the ebooks I downloaded from Amazon rely on variations of the same few techniques. The finished outlines tend to create books without depth, largely because they are almost entirely event-driven.

In the end, I went away for a week with a notepad and a

laptop to try and work out a new way of outlining. On the third morning, I'd just drained my first coffee of the day, when I had one of those *lightbulb moments*. Something James Patterson had said resonated with an idea I'd just jotted down, and I was pretty sure I'd made a breakthrough.

Four hours later, I'd managed to construct a detailed outline of my detailed trilogy.

Phew!

The technique I came up with is what I'm going to show you here. It's not completely revolutionary or totally unlike what's gone before, but it is different. I've knocked off a few rough edges and simplified some of the processes. I'm sure it'll work just as well for you as it does for me.

Who This Book Is For

MY METHOD of outlining will work for practically every author in any genre, from Literary to Erotica, via Horror, SF, Mystery, Space Punk, and Young Adult. Having said that, the more plot there is, the better the system will work.

Although it is still possible to outline a 'stream of consciousness' novel, it's much easier when you're dealing with a series of well-defined events.

On the whole, authors writing 'commercial fiction' need to work from an outline. Commercial fiction is another way of talking about writing that is designed to be popular. It might be a Detective story, a Romance, a Zombie Thriller, or Chick-Lit. By its very nature, commercial fiction will always dominate the bestseller lists.

The two crucial factors in any popular work of fiction are story and character. The two should be interwoven like strands of a rope. A major part of the storytelling process involves outlining how characters behave inside a story.

I'm confident that anyone who writes with that in mind will benefit from reading this book.

The Brutal Truths Concerning Commercial Fiction

WRITING for money is nothing to be ashamed of. If you opened up a restaurant designed to repel potential diners, people would think you were mad but, for some reason, writing novels most potential readers wouldn't enjoy is seen as a worthy occupation.

Many modern authors, including James Patterson, Lee Child, and Mark Billingham, deliberately started writing in order to earn a living. As did the likes of Charles Dickens, Agatha Christie, and Dashiell Hammett, before them. No one looks down on well-paid architects or film directors, but somehow authors (and painters) are supposed to feel guilty if they ever make a decent living. I give you full permission not to worry about how much you can potentially earn from your writing.

Commercial novelists thrive and prosper by giving readers what they want. As thousands of authors, including Raymond Chandler, William Boyd, JD Sallinger, Ross Macdonald, James Ellroy, Elmore Leonard, JK Rowling, Patricia Highsmith, and John Irving, have shown, it is possible to be both a good writer and commercially successful at the same time.

The obvious way to be successful is to look at what's selling and write something similar but better. I'm not suggesting you copy any other author's work. On the contrary, one of the secrets of a well-outlined novel is to avoid duplicating anything commonplace or cliched.

Plotters vs Pantsers

THE AIM of the commercial novelist should be to always create the best story you possibly can. You want to start with a bang and fashion every chapter so that it makes the reader want to move on to the next. Clever plot twists are woven into the action. The reader finds themselves constantly surprised and delighted. As they close the last page, the reader should be thinking, *Wow, what a great story!*

Of course, that's easier said than done.

As you probably know, there are two basic types of author: the *outliner* and the *pantser*. Some novelists — especially beginners — still insist on making up stories as they go along. They say things like, "I want to feel my characters come alive," and, "I let my protagonist tell me where the story's going." This technique is called 'pantsing' (from *flying by the seat of your pants*) and usually involves the author spending many months slaving over countless drafts in order to come up with a workable story.

Authors who make things up as they go along invariably throw away more words than they end up using. And, just like Stephen King, they're actually creating an outline inside their heads by the most labour intensive method possible.

Outlining makes the job of storytelling so much easier. If you're writing by the *seat of your pants* method, you'll be bogged down in action you might very well end up having to ditch. Every new twist or turn you think of will probably involve rewriting whole chapters of what you've already sweated over.

Outlining a novel is like taking a trip using a map or sat-nav. The alternative is to rely on your instincts. Why would you set off on any journey not knowing where you're going or which roads you're going to take? You might make it in the end, but why put yourself through the hardship?

Making it up as you go along is very labour-intensive and, believe me, can lead to dead-end after dead-end. I really don't want to write 10,000 or more words before I realise that there's some horrible glitch that makes the story fall apart. To my mind, a detailed outline can highlight 99.99% of these problems.

The author George RR Martin of *Game of Thrones* fame is a well-known *pantser*. That's probably why it takes him literally years and years to write each and every volume. I'd guess that if he spent more time working on his outlines and less time trying to 'wing it,' we'd be on volume 25 of the *Ice and Fire* series by now.

What Is Plot?

PEOPLE GET CONFUSED about plot and story. Many of them seem to think they are the same thing. Sometimes they can be but, more often than not, they're different.

The majority of those who call themselves experts in story structure say stuff like, 'Plot is structure,' which is another way of saying that plot is the scaffolding on which a story can hang. *Chambers Concise Dictionary* defines plot as: "The story or scheme of connected events running through a play, novel, etc." That's their *etc*, not mine.

Plot is the *he did this, she did that,* aspect of story. It's a sequence of events put in a certain order. A character who kills someone without provocation is a murderer. The same character who stumbles in on home-invaders torturing his wife and children would not be blamed for trying to defend them. How you order events can be crucial to the story's meaning.

Plot moves the story forward and adds to the suspense. Notice the expression, *moves the story forward*, which couldn't possibly happen if plot and story were the same.

What Is Story?

THE *OXFORD ENGLISH Dictionary* defines STORY as:

An account of imaginary or real people and events told
for entertainment: an adventure story | I'm going to tell
you a story.

a storyline: *the novel has a good story.*

a piece of gossip; a rumour: *there have been lots of
stories going around, as you can imagine.*

informal a false statement; a lie: *Ellie never* **told stories**
—she had always believed in the truth.

Most people find it surprising that the dictionary defini-
tion of a story is that it has to be made up. It cannot be real-
life and a lie is counted as a story.

True stories invariably have to be adapted in drastic ways to
make them acceptable to readers and viewers looking for a satisfactory story. Real-life has a nasty habit of not being believable.

You'd be amazed how often writers of fiction have to

change real events because no one would believe they actually happened and, anyway, factual events usually take place in the wrong order.

In fiction, detectives can say things like, "I don't believe in coincidences." Real life cops have to deal with coincidence all day, every day. The craft of the writer is to construct a story that is both believable and interesting to the reader. That involves creating a world of fiction that has little to do with the everyday world.

To appear realistic, fiction has to be carefully crafted to give the impression of realism. If authors depicted how people really behaved and spoke in real life, it'd be boring. People stutter, talk nonsense and ramble. Part of the craft of story is creating a world in which characters act and speak as if they're being realistic but are actually anything but.

Although their creators prided themselves on so-called realism, if classic TV shows like *Hill Street Blues*, *The Wire*, and *Homicide: Life on the Street*, had been forced to rely only on true cases acted out the way they really went down, they'd have been in all kinds of trouble. They would certainly not have gone on to become cult classics. That they succeeded at all is thanks to clever writing.

Movies that start with the caption, 'Based on real events,' have been turned into fiction by groups of writers. In real life, people do things for no logical reason, they act on impulse, and coincidence abounds. That's why writers have to use their skills to construct stories — and 'adapt' real life events into a narrative that's believable.

Stories Need Structure

When a friend tells you about an elderly neighbour who's just passed away, that's not a story, that's an event. When you hear that the same person died of a broken heart the day after his wife of sixty years was killed by a hit-and-run driver, that's the basis for a story.

To make a story interesting, it needs:

1. STRUCTURE: Beginning, Middle, and End.
2. INTERESTING things need to happen. In the writing world, this is often called CONFLICT. Characters battling for opposing goals.
3. CHARACTERS people care about.
4. SURPRISE. Events must take UNEXPECTED turns. It gets boring if everything proceeds according to plan.
5. RESOLUTION. Some kind of satisfactory ending.

To turn this around, let's look at a story from the viewpoint of the lead character. You'll notice that the same five elements are present, but we are looking at the story from a different angle:

1. The lead character (or characters) have a goal they need to achieve…
2. They are opposed…
3. They suffer advances and setbacks…
4. Until they either succeed or fail at winning their objective.

That simple summation of story covers almost every novel or movie you care to mention, from *Lord of The Rings* and *Black Panther* to *The Da Vinci Code*, *Casablanca*, even *Fifty Shades of Grey*. Other elements help make a story more rounded and more organic but this simple structure has been the basis of almost every successful piece of fiction since the novel was first formulated in the eighteenth century.

Story Is Not Just About Plot

Despite what many people assume, outlining cannot just be about plot. As we've already seen, a plot is a series of incidents involving characters. To be perceived as realistic, your characters have to be seen to react and change according to what's going on around them. A gunman robbing a store is an event that will have consequences for everyone involved: for the robber as well as the victims.

How characters react to an event have the power to propel the story forward just as much as the event itself. The man who is forced to take extreme action to rescue his wife from kidnappers is not going to be the same person afterward. Plenty of fiction is about ordinary people who are forced to behave in extraordinary ways. For the story to make sense, that person has to be seen to change, and the way he or she changes should help to push the story forward.

When you create a story, you are inventing a complete world. It helps to create this type of 'realism' by organic methods. A series of muggings or violent robberies in a neighbourhood, for instance, will lead to the residents becoming more edgy and less trusting of strangers.

They might rush home straight after work, stay in their homes more, travel in pairs. Stores will increase security, maybe more cops will be moved into the area. The cops will be looking out for gunmen and so will be less relaxed in the way they work. These subtle but important changes should be considered within a story outline.

Beware Of Rigid Story Structure

If you search online, you can find hundreds of so-called 'story templates' for writers to use. Some of them sound as if they've been stolen from some kind of Victorian Gothic Horror handbook. Here's an example:

ACT ONE

1. The Ordinary World
2. Inciting Incident
3. The Call To Adventure
4. The Lock In

ACT TWO

1. Tests & Trials
2. First Failure
3. The Midpoint
4. Major Setback
5. All Hope Is Lost

ACT THREE

1. Inspiring Incident
2. Girding The Loins
3. Climax (Final Battle)

Writing by numbers like this works for some, but it's not something I'd recommend. I like the idea of 'girding the loins,' but I'm not so keen on following a rigid framework that doesn't take into account the complexities of an individual story. In most cases, it'd be like trying to stuff an elephant into a penguin suit.

Now we know what a story is (and what it isn't), we can start to construct our own. Outlining commercial fiction certainly isn't the simplest task you'll ever attempt but my method makes it far easier than you'd expect. The prospect certainly shouldn't scare you.

Let's jump right in…

First Steps

How We're Going To Do This...

ONCE WE HAVE a basic story idea, we can start the outlining process. I like to work in easy stages. Where many would-be plotters go wrong is that they try and achieve too much, too soon.

When I was formulating my outlining plan, it didn't take long to work out I had to make story decisions in a logical order. To try and decide who my protagonist was before I knew the period and location in which the story was taking place was stupid. A novel set in Victorian London would have vastly different options available to one set in the dystopian future.

As I keep saying, when you are creating an outline, you can change your mind about anything at any stage. That's why I love outlining so much and why I pity the poor *pantsers*. These guys have to go back and rewrite thousands of words for every tiny improvement they want to make. I'll bet lots of great ideas never see the light of day simply because these fatheads can't be bothered to rewrite everything they've already written. We, on the other hand, get to change a few words here and there anytime we like.

My method involves working through six distinct stages:

1. Who's it for?
2. Overview
3. Ultimate aims
4. Character progression
5. The Premise
6. Character outlines

Before we can get started, we need the bones of a basic story. We've got to know what's going to happen, when, and to whom.

How I Like To Work

Writing stuff down in longhand seems easiest for me, at least in these early stages of outlining. I use a big lined pad and I write in well-spaced, bullet-point type notes, mixing my neatest handwriting with block capitals and underlining for emphasis. I like using coloured pens, too.

They do say that the act of physically writing words down onto paper helps the brain absorb information. It certainly helped me when I was studying for school and university exams all those years ago.

When I'm happy with what I've got, I move to the computer, referring to my handwritten notes for guidance. The app I use at this stage of the outlining process is the bog standard word processing software that came with my computer: in my case, Pages for Mac.

I write very much as I would when I'm writing the finished novel. Fast and with the minimum of pauses. This helps me concentrate and I get more done.

For the final stages of outlining and for the whole of the writing process, I switch to a program called Scrivener. I don't earn anything by referring students to this amazing software, but the link should get you a free trial.

A large number of writers use Scrivener, simply because

it's really a uniquely useful tool. This is not the place for a long tutorial about how Scrivener works or what it does, but I'll just say I'm working in Scrivener right now.0

A Little About Scrivener

This next bit won't mean much to people who don't know about Scrivener, but those who do may find it useful. In the Binder, I create a file for each chapter, and I usually put these inside folders for Act 1, Act 2, Act 3. This has no major significance, it's just for my own use and to keep things tidy.

When I come to write the novel, I write the chapters in order using Scrivener. First of all, I go to the Inspector and type in the synopsis of that particular chapter. Having done this, everything that's about to happen in the chapter is fresh in my mind when I start writing. The internet and phones are all switched off and I don't stop until it's done. As my chapters tend to be quite short, I aim to write five in a day. I try not to edit or correct much as I write. That comes later.

When I've finished the day's chapters, I go for a walk, have lunch, or do something else for an hour or so. Then I come back and run over what I've written, making corrections and checking that everything flows nicely. That's usually the end of my writing day.

Creating A Workable Idea

I'M ASSUMING you already have a rough idea for a story. If not, you need to find one. For help thinking up ideas, another of my books, *How To Write A Novel The Easy Way*, suggests a ton of ways you can go about it. It's free to download from most (though not all) Amazon stores.

The very first thing to decide on is the genre in which you want to write. I suggest you go for something you read yourself and that you personally enjoy. If you like Mystery books and can't stand Sci-fi, I think you'd be silly to write a futurist novel set on a space station in 2516.

One of the main advantages of writing in a genre you already know is that you'll be aware of ideas that are considered clichéd and commonplace. The alcoholic detective with a failed marriage certainly should be avoided, unless you can genuinely find a new angle that will make the story interesting and fresh. Someone who has never read a detective novel or seen a movie would have no idea how many times this type of character has cropped up over the years.

Writing in a genre you are familiar with also means you'll be aware of reader expectation. In its simplest form, this means a mystery novel should feature a detective of some kind, that vampires ought to be predatory blood-seekers, and that Romance novels need to employ some kind of emotional tension.

Making a novel fresh and interesting whilst living up to reader expectations can be a tricky balancing act. Familiarity with a genre and its 'classics' makes you aware of possibilities, whilst stopping you from straying too far from what the readers expect.

If you want to write a cozy mystery, by all means, set it in an English country village, but try and find a new and interesting angle. Maybe your detective could be the barmaid in the village pub. *Has that ever been done?* Perhaps the vicar is an imposter who strangled the real incumbent and took over his role?

You could change the time and location: how about a cozy mystery set in New Hampshire in the 1950s, or in China during the Boxer Rebellion? I really think I'd like to read an Agatha Christie-style murder mystery set in rural France during the German Occupation. Has anyone done that?

You've got to think outside the box, without ever straying too far from what your potential readers will accept. We'll look more closely at 'reader targeting' in a later chapter but, for now, it's important your overall idea is at least commercially viable. We know you can't please all the people all the time, but the last thing you need right now is for your basic idea to alienate most of your potential audience.

Inexperienced authors often slip up when they try to be 'too clever' by combining genres. Although a very few experienced writers have managed to achieve some success by doing so, the vast majority of books and movies that attempt to put cowboys and aliens together, or zombies with World War II Nazis, have failed miserably. People who enjoy a cozy mystery of the Agatha Christie type, simply don't want to find out it was an alien from the planet Zog who murdered Lord Edgware.

Gradually Adding Detail

AT THIS STAGE we're just looking for ideas, so your central concept doesn't have to be very elaborate. It could be something as simple as:

A detective must stop a serial killer before he murders his (the detective's) wife and daughter; or, *Aliens land on earth and take over a secret government research centre.*

These ideas are pretty basic and there's no hint of time or place. Taking the first scenario as an example, I would find a piece of paper (or a computer), and write down:

1. *General idea:* A detective must stop a serial killer before he murders his wife and daughter.
2. *Time and place:*

Step 2

The location and timeframe can be literally anything you decide on. London in 1888, New York in the present day, Dallas in November 1963. It could be China, India, or Germany. 1944, 1776, or 2025. The possibilities are practically infinite. You can choose the past, the present, or the future. The location could be anywhere on earth, or even beyond it. The only restraints are the conventions of your chosen genre.

Let's plump for London in the present day. Our *Outline Rough* would look like this:

1. *General idea:* A detective must stop a serial killer before he murders his wife and daughter.
2. *Time and place:* London, present day.

Remember, we are not yet working on the outline itself. We are gathering information we are going to use to create one.

Adding Basic Characters

I'M GUESSING you'll have some idea of who your lead character is going to be. In the case of the detective scenario, it'll obviously be a detective. Does he/she work for the police or are they private?

Let's make her a woman. You can always change her sex later if this doesn't work out. *(In a previous edition, the detective was male, so it shows how easy it is to be flexible!)*

If she's a police detective, what rank? What does she investigate (homicides, fires, theft, general crime in a borough, etc)?, and where?

You'll find that conventions of the character's occupation will often limit your choices. For example, it's unlikely you'll find a detective working for the police who's under twenty or over sixty, and they'll rarely put a teenage recruit in charge of a murder investigation.

Similarly, if you're writing a novel about professional fashion models, there's invariably an upper age cut-off point. Combat troops and college footballers are generally fit young men. Retired people tend to be sixty and over.

Once you have your lead character, it's a small step to add the people who would be close to him or her. Spouse, children, bosses, co-workers, and so on. You don't have to be extensive here, just include the people you think might make it into the story. I'll say it again: *don't worry if you get it exactly right, the important thing is to take action, even if you have to delete or edit later.*

In the case of the detective in our initial scenario, we might come up with:

Detective Chief Inspector Stephanie ('Stevie') Simpson *(42 years old) is based at Lewisham Police Station in London, where she works under* **Superintendent Alan Wise**, *in the South East Regional Murder Squad. She lives in nearby Blackheath with her husband,* **Carl** *(39), and daughter* **Abigail** *(14). Key members of her team include* **Detective Sergeant Jaspreet Gill** *and* **Detective Constable Colin Dexter**.

So far, so good…

Now, we need an antagonist. The serial killer who is eventually going to threaten to murder Steve's husband and daughter. Let's call him 'The Stripper,' real name Ronald Morgan, and make him a lawyer, for no reason other than that was the first thought that came into my mind.

Our Rough Outline might now look something like this:

General idea: A detective must stop a serial killer before he murders his husband and daughter.

Time and place: London, present day.

Lead character: **Detective Chief Inspector Stephanie ('Stevie') Simpson** *(42 years old) is based at Lewisham Police Station in London, where she works under* **Superintendent Alan Wise**, *in the South East Regional Murder Squad. She* *lives in nearby Blackheath with her husband, **Carl** (39), and daughter **Abigail** (14). Key members of her team include* **Detective Sergeant Jaspreet Gill** *and* **Detective Constable Colin Dexter**.

Antagonist: **'The Stripper,'** real name **Ronald Morgan**, a barrister working out of Gray's Inn, in central London.

That didn't take long, did it?

Alternative Scenario

I'VE JUST SHOWN you one way to come up with the bones of a plot you can use to write a novel. Here's another.

Just to show you how simple this method is, I'll quickly pull together a scenario from thin air. I promise you I've prepared nothing in advance, and I'm putting it down exactly as I think of it.

To get me started, I'm going to the Amazon Kindle ebook Best Sellers page: here's a link. On the day I visited, the list of the biggest selling ebooks on the site looked like this:

A book that caught my eye was *The Prettiest One* by James Hankins. Partly because it was published and available to buy (unlike the top 5, which were due for publication around a month after my search), plus it wasn't a straight-up Mystery story like most of the others.

Although Amazon doesn't reveal sales figures to anyone other than the publisher, it's estimated that the number 9 bestseller will sell around 100,000 copies a month. That's just ebook downloads, printed paperback and hardback sales are on top. For books priced at $2.99 and over, Amazon pays 70% royalties, so at $5.99 each, that'll work out to quite a sum.

I usually look at the customer reviews to find out what a book is *really* about. I've found that the synopsis provided by the publisher inevitably provides more sales jargon than information. The first review I took a note of was from KristinaS, who said:

I read this book in one sitting. From the first two pages until the very end, I couldn't put it down. The writing was fast paced and gave just enough information about the characters to allow the reader to infer a lot more. The mystery held up well throughout and each chapter had some new twist or surprise that kept me wanting more. A few mysteries never did get answered but that makes it even more interesting and memorable. It's a hard one to review without spoilers so I'll stop here and suggest that people avoid reading too many of the reviews in advance because the unwarned spoilers take away from the enjoyment of the book.

As a writer, this gave me clues as to how the author had structured the book. I took note of what was said and looked for a more detailed synopsis. The most comprehensive one I came across was from Judith D. Collins. Her review is long (over 1,200 words) but it does provide some great insight for anyone considering writing a book within the same genre:

James Hankins returns following the popular *Shady Cross* with a psychological mystery crime suspense page-turner, The Prettiest One —a memory wiped out, a decades-old crime, a race against time, and two men risking it all, to save the woman they both love.

Caitlin Sommers, a real estate agent finds herself in a fog. She has no idea of the time, date, or where she is. Everything is hazy. She recalled going to a store and buying something yellow. She is in a strange place and does not recognise how she arrived.

She gets in a strange car and is almost on audio-pilot. She thinks her husband is Josh and she begins driving, not really sure where she is or where she is going. No cellphone. However, she makes her way home to Bristol, New Hampshire a few hours away. Nothing makes sense.

When she arrives home, Josh is so glad to see his wife. He is beyond shocked. She has been missing for seven months.

She now is wearing different clothes and her hair is red instead of blonde. She has also lost weight and has a bad haircut. She has no clue where she has been for seven months. No memory at all. She is unaware they suspected Josh of foul play since the authorities have been unable to locate her. Everyone has been frantically searching for her. She also has blood on her clothes but does not seem to be hurt.

She is exhausted, goes to bed and they decide the next day they will search for answers, and try and figure out whose car she has stolen. She will go back the way she came if she can remember and try and find why she was in another town and what she had been doing. She needs to put the pieces of the puzzle together.

However, when they get to the car, there is a bag, a gun and a bag of prosthetic hands. Instead of going to the police, she wants to find answers first. Did she kill someone? Why is she driving a car registered to Katherine Southard?

In the desperate search, they discover Caitlin was going by another name, Katie, and she was living with a guy named Bix, and they were engaged in Massachusetts. She had a job and was living a separate life. She has no memory of knowing this man.

The three of them (Caitlin, Josh, and Bix) begin an intriguing journey, a mystery, a dangerous past. Josh did not want to return to the place his wife had been, as possibly it was something so tragic, she has blocked it out. However, he goes along with her wishes. Why was she in Smithfield, Massachusetts? If she had committed a crime, the police would be looking for her.

Caitlin/Katie has experienced bad ongoing

nightmares of the Bogeyman for years. It was the same nightmare she since she was little. He always said, "I've got you, my pretty Caitlin." He was gross, His eyes, his hands, his rotting smell like garbage. Who is this monster? Could he be real? What happened to her in her childhood?

In the meantime, there is another character, Chops, who kills people in his garage. He has a wife and young daughter, under the appearance of a hard working construction owner and family man. An evil hit man and he is trying to locate another man. Until later in the book, you are unaware how he is connected.

Josh, Bix, and Caitlin/Katie find themselves in the middle of a crime, several murders, and a dangerous plot from years ago when the past and the present collide.

Why would Caitlin drive to another town and have a normal life with someone else, and be unable to recall that life? People have been murdered, and they are led to these rough bars and basement fight clubs, and appears Katie was a regular customer. What was she doing in these places? Now she is somewhat of a mystery to both Josh and Bix. Who is this woman and who is out to get her and why?

The more online research Josh conducts, he discovers Caitlin may have dissociative fugue; whereby, a person not only loses their memory and the knowledge of herself, but she might travel to a new place and set up an entirely new identity somewhere. Which is exactly what she did.

The condition could be triggered by extreme stress or trauma. A person could wander off. It can last as short as a few hours, a day, months, or years. They establish new relationships. No one seems to know exactly what makes them come out of a fugue state. It could be seeing something small or something that reminds them enough of their former life. Or some experts think that a traumatic event of some kind could snap a person out, especially if it somehow relates to whatever put them in that state in the first place.

As the layers are peeled back, more hidden sadistic acts are uncovered, and Detective Charlotte Hunnsaker is on the case and is clueless. There is a warehouse shooting, a murder, a red head, and fingerprints and a long-ago kidnapping, an abduction, a pedophile. How are all these elements connected?

Aside from the crimes, evil men, and the mystery, you are dying to know which man, if either, Caitlin/Katie will choose when this is over. Who will survive? And if Caitlin will end up behind bars?

One thing about James Hankins -- you are always surprised—having read all his books, each one is unique, creative, and different. He always hooks you from the beginning, keeping you in suspense--you never know what is coming next.

What I enjoyed about *The Prettiest One*, was the banter between Josh and Bix; the relationship dynamics also between the three. All three characters were well-developed. Two totally different guys, both in love with the same girl, and Caitlin/Katie was almost like two different people, with her wide range of personalities.

James did a super job with the wit, emotion, intensity, humour, and frustration of the two guys in this love triangle mystery. One life was more conservative; whereas, the other more on the wild side. How the guys stuck together for the greater cause, to help find the killer, and protect Caitlin was a strong part of the storyline.

The Dissociative Fugue, like episodes of amnesia, was quite intriguing. Hankins used a nice spin, connecting all the storylines. Have read there are rare cases when a person is still in the fugue, recovering information is critical (with help from law enforcement or social services) about his/her true identity, figuring out why they were abandoned, and facilitating its restoration is key.

For you psycho-thriller fans, the most powerful part of the thriller was the kidnapping years ago of the three girls, the sadistic man, and family involved in the present story. Recommended for those readers who enjoy a slow burning complex crime mystery with a psycho-evil twist.

Fans of Chevy Stevens and Karin Slaughter will enjoy (when you read, you will know the parts I am referring to).

I'll be honest and admit it's not often you'll find a customer review that will be quite as useful to a writer as this one. The reviewer is obviously experienced in critiquing novels and she essentially performs an autopsy on the novel and points out what she liked and what she didn't like. Most importantly, she explains why. Customer reviews can be extremely useful to writers because they reveal what average readers think about the books they are reading.

Here I'll strike a note of caution. When you're reading reviews, it's important to remember that what you're reading is one person's opinion. Sometimes the best and most articulate review will be out of step with what everyone else is saying. You have to go with the majority.

∽

BEFORE WE GO ANY FURTHER, let me get one thing straight: we are not going to copy James Hankins or his thriller in any way. We are using his premise to work on ideas of our own.

I have a feeling this is something James has already done himself, as *The Prettiest One* came hot on the heels of 'amnesia thriller' bestsellers like Gillian Flynn's *Gone Girl,* and *Girl on the Train* by Paula Hawkins. At least James didn't use the word 'girl' in his title. The success of all these novels assures us that there is a lively market awaiting our own effort.

The first thing I'm going to change is the sex of the main character. Let's make him a man who wakes up not remembering his past. That will make it fundamentally different, for a start. Let's also shift the location and time-scale from the USA today to… World War II England.

Why? *Because we can!*

It could just as easily have been modern-day Africa, Renaissance-era Florence, or Dublin in 1922. As I say, the possibilities are endless.

Having decided on a time and a place, I might fill in the first two steps of my Rough Outline like this:

General idea: A man wakes up in a bombed building in London's docklands, not knowing who he is or how he got there. Inside his pocket is an envelope containing 20,000 German Reichsmarks.

Time and place: London, 1944.

You'll notice I added the twist of the German currency. I also had an idea that he was thinking in German, but that's just a notion that can wait for the next stage. As Britain was at war with Hitler's Germany in 1944, this makes for a potentially interesting scenario.

Because our process demands we know where 'the man' (our lead character) comes from, it's time to work on his identity straight away. When we come to outline, we won't be revealing anything like as much information to our readers until much later in the novel.

Although there's still a lot to work out, we can say:

General idea: A man wakes up in a bombed building in London's docklands, not knowing who he is or how he got there. Inside his pocket is an envelope containing 20,000 German Reichsmarks.

Time and place: London, 1944.

Lead character: **Desmond Johnson**, a German-speaking British architect who is working undercover for MI5 during World War II. He awakes in the house in docklands after returning from Germany after a very difficult mission in which he was captured and tortured. He escaped and made his way to London. The British have been told by American Intelligence that Johnson has 'turned' and is now a danger to the Allied Cause, This is untrue.

Antagonists: I've decided there will be two: **General Van Dorff** in Berlin, who has sworn to destroy Johnson; and **US Colonel Steve Austin** in London, who genuinely believes Johnson is a double agent.

There are lots of questions still to be answered, but I'm really quite pleased with the kernel of the story we've managed to pluck out of thin air. There's no question of plagiarism because our story is completely different to the one we looked to for inspiration. The only common denominator is 'amnesia,' and that's not even been medically diagnosed yet!

Now We Are Ready To Outline

ONCE WE GET to this stage, we are well on our way to creating a great outline. I can't tell you how rewarding it was for me to reach this point when I was outlining my Detective trilogy.

I may have subconsciously 'known' most of what I'd worked out already, but to see it written down and presented in this way made me realise my novels were just a few steps away from being written and published.

The important thing about outlining is to stay flexible. As I keep stressing, you are undoubtedly going to make significant changes to what you've already decided, that's inevitable. It's all about taking and improving until your outline can get no better.

Second Steps

Who Are You Writing For?

THE BIG SECRET I took away from the James Patterson Masterclass was that he writes with a particular reader in mind. In his case, it's a generic middle-aged woman who lives somewhere in the USA. Let's call her 'Sharon', a name that is purely my own invention.

Patterson doesn't go into any great detail about Sharon. I'm guessing he commissioned research that identified the type of person most likely to buy his books, and he's keeping that kind of information close to his chest. Before becoming a writer, James was a high-powered advertising executive, so you can bet he knows his way around a focus group report.

At every stage of the writing process, from deciding on a story to plotting and finally getting the words down, James revealed that he asks himself how his target reader would react to whatever it is he's planning to do.

Would Sharon approve of the novel's hero? If not, how could he make him more likeable to her? Should he include an explicit torture scene or would Sharon prefer something less graphic? And so on…

You can see now how important this mythical Sharon

figure might be. Making a hero attractive to her might involve making him ex-military, gung-ho patriotic, and perhaps a little conservative. To make a character attractive to a male shoemaker in Cairo or to a waiter in Paris would involve a totally different thought process.

At this point, many new writers despair. "How on earth can I discover who's most likely to buy my book or watch my finished movie?" Luckily, most of what you have to do involves nothing more than a little research and a dollop of old-fashioned common sense.

Writing for a particular market is nothing new. Authors of juvenile fiction have always done it, as have those specialising in Romance and Westerns. Young adult fiction is obviously written for people under a certain age, and only an idiot would think that the typical reader of War stories would be a ninety-five-year-old grandma.

As we already know, the best way to satisfy any audience is to give them what they want. This involves meeting the expectations of the genre you are writing in. Working out a more specific idea of who you are writing for is another side of the same coin. It's just a matter of putting a human face onto an abstract concept.

Don't worry, you don't need to be 100% accurate or scientific to see results. No one will die if you get it slightly wrong. If discovering who you are writing for takes too much time or puts a block in the way of the writing process, then you must be doing it wrong. The idea is for it to help you, not hold you back.

I start by using my common sense. If I'm writing a Detective novel, what type of Detective novel is it? People who read PD James's detective stories will be different to those who read the novels of Ross MacDonald or James Ellroy. Fans of Locked Room Mysteries are probably not the same people who crave S&M Erotic Romances — though you never can tell!

Once I am aware of my story's genre, I narrow it down even further. I find two or three authors in the Amazon Bestseller lists who are writing roughly the same kind of fiction. It may take a while but the effort will invariably pay off. I browse in Bestsellers because this is basically a list of books by the world's most successful authors at the present time.

By reading customer reviews of novels by these authors, I get an idea of who is buying them. The people who find the time to review can be classed as 'super interested' and these are the ones I want to find out about.

The reviews — good and bad — give an idea of who the author's readers are and what they are like. Very few of them will say stuff like, "I'm a forty-year-old man from Wisconsin who lives with his mother and works in a library." It is up to you to use your author's instincts. This is not a scientific exercise: you are building up a profile of an imaginary person based on feedback from many different readers. There is no right and no wrong.

Slowly but surely, I get an idea of who my target reader is likely to be. I find it fun to give him or her a name and identity, but you don't have to. I ask myself questions like, "What would Stanley think about this?" and, "Would Elizabeth accept that this needs to be done?" At the same time, I am fully aware that Stanley and Elizabeth do not exist. They are an amalgam of many different people. Tools that will help me keep my fiction consistent and 'on target'.

Ideally, no one outside the writing process would be able to work out who my ideal reader is. Until I heard the words come out of his mouth, I had no idea who James Patterson was writing for, even though I've read many of his books.

On the other hand, some authors do very well by making it obvious who their target audience is and going all out to attract them. For instance, they might decide to appeal to male patriots in the USA and write about characters who reflect the values of their target reader. There's certainly a market for this kind of fiction.

Whatever you decide, it's your call.

Overview

THE FOUR PARAGRAPHS we created a little while ago — *General idea, Time and place, Lead character,* and *Antagonists* — provide us with practically all the information we need to create the first draft of the Overview of our outline. All we have to do is convert the information that's already in place — maybe adding a little more detail — into one or two paragraphs of text.

You'll remember that the Detective story began as a vague idea, to which we gradually added information as we worked it out. This is the next stage of the same process. Every time we work on the overview, we get to add more and more detail. The time has come to let your imagination run loose.

In the case of the Detective story, I might write:

A serial killer called **The Stripper** is on the loose in southeast London, preying on attractive young women who live alone. He traps them in their home, strangles them, before removing their clothes, and laying them out in poses reminiscent of strippers.

Leading the Murder Squad assigned to investigating

The Stripper is **Detective Chief Inspector Stephanie 'Stevie' Simpson**, who is 42 years old, and lives in Blackheath with her husband, **Carl** (39), and daughter **Abigail** (14). Due to bullying at school, Stevie lacks self-belief and frequently suffers from panic attacks. So far, she has managed to keep this from her colleagues in the police.

Stevie's boss is **Superintendent Alan Wise** (53), and they are based at Lewisham Police Station. Steve's number two in his squad is **Detective Sergeant Jaspreet Gill** (36), an ambitious career detective (female) of Sikh faith, and **Detective Constable Colin Dexter** (26), a thorough but less-than-inspiring detective who does everything by the book. Although they seldom put their thoughts into words, Wise and members of his team are silently resentful that Stevie is a poor delegator who prefers to work alone.

There is an indication that the killer is receiving inside information about the investigation, which points to a 'mole' inside the police. Thanks to a tip-off (NOTE: how did that come about???), Stevie almost catches The Stripper in action, but he escapes and threatens to attack and kill the DCI's husband and daughter unless she backs off. Does Stevie tell anyone about the threats and so risk her family's life, or does she work alone to catch the murderer?

The story is advancing nicely. All the extra information was achieved by converting what we already knew into this different format and making up a little more detail here and there. We still don't know how the story will end, but that'll come soon enough. Whenever I don't know the answer to a specific plot point, I add a 'NOTE' to myself using three ??? to make searching easy.

The 1944 Amnesia scenario might go something like this:

A man awakes alone in a bombed-out house in wartime London. He cannot remember who he is and has no memory of his past life. Although he feels he might be British, he is alarmed to have German words and phrases rattling around in his head. Perhaps he is a spy?

The reader gradually discovers he is **Captain Desmond Johnson**, a former architect who has been working undercover in Germany for MI5. On his last mission he was discovered and tortured by the Gestapo, only escaping by the skin of his teeth (NOTE: how???). There is a suspicion he was allowed to escape. How he reached the house in London is currently a mystery.

Johnson can trust no one. The Germans are after him, and his US nemesis, **Colonel Steve Austin**, has convinced his British bosses that he has turned. Johnson has to clear his name and discover what happened between his capture in Berlin and his waking up in the bombed house in London.

There are still plenty of questions that need answering and gaps to be filled but when you consider that an hour ago, we didn't have any idea of a plot or story, I think we've done pretty well. This is definitely the type of story I'd like to read myself.

Stage 2 of the outlining process is called 'Ultimate Aims'. It will help us fill in more of the gaps.

Ultimate Aims

IN ORDER TO create a believable story, a writer must know what it is that motivates each of the central characters. This entails working out their **ultimate aims**. The UA is not a character's goal in life but what they are striving for within the confines of the story.

An accountant may have a life goal of making a million and being able to retire before he reaches fifty, but if we are writing about the kidnapping of his wife, all we are concerned with is his ultimate aim as far as it affects the story, which to secure her release.

Occasionally the life goal and the UA can be the same thing. In *Breaking Bad*, Walter's ultimate aim soon becomes clear: to use his knowledge of chemistry to secure a financial future for his family following his inevitable death from lung cancer. That explains why a mild-mannered school chemistry teacher ignores the ethical and moral codes he has lived his life by, and moves into the murky world of drug manufacturing and dealing,.

For the UA to work successfully, it must be easily defined. That means, being able to write it down as a single sentence.

It must be specific: there's no room for fudge or haziness. If a character's wife and daughter have been murdered in a drive-by shooting and you write, 'he wants the killers punished', that would be too vague. If you delve deeper, you might decide his ultimate aim would be: 'To discover the identities of his wife and daughter's killers by careful detective work, and bring them to justice.' Or maybe, 'To find and kill the people who were responsible for murdering his wife and children.'

The important thing to remember is that we are only concerned with the UA in as much as it affects the story we are writing. Sometimes it can be as simple as, 'To make Miss Kubelik love me and want to marry me.'

Give The Lead An Impediment

The *impediment* is a trick of the trade used by many successful authors. It involves giving the central character some kind of failing or handicap that can be incorporated into his or her ultimate aim.

By impediment, I mean something that will make it harder — or seemingly impossible — for them to succeed in their UA. Maybe the husband is shown to have a fear of guns at the beginning of the story. In which case, his ultimate aim would be, 'To overcome his fear of firearms and find and kill the people who were responsible for murdering his wife and children.'

The lead character's impediment doesn't have to be anything too obvious or life-threatening, but it does need to be something that can be overcome. A war veteran with no arms or legs couldn't realistically end up playing for the main Harlem Globetrotters basketball team, but someone with a bad stutter might conceivably be cured and end up hosting a radio show.

It's not always what you expect. Walt's impediment in *Breaking Bad*, for example, was not his terminal cancer, but the family's lack of money.

In the case of our detective battling against The Stripper, on the face of it, Steve Simpson's ultimate aim might be, 'To bring The Stripper to justice and ensure the safety of his wife and daughter.' But that doesn't take account of what Steve's impediment might be. There are literally thousands of options. He could be a secret drug addict, or he might be haunted by visions of people who have died (as in the BBC TV series *River*), or maybe he has crippling attacks of self-doubt.

In this case, I've decided to go with the panic attacks. This would mean his UA would read, 'To overcome his crippling self-doubt and bring The Stripper to justice to ensure the safety of his wife and daughter.' That's not a very pretty sentence, but it makes sense, and no one but you is going to be reading it.

If you find yourself with a *very* convoluted sentence, you'll need to work on it until you have something useable. It is important that you, as the writer, are entirely clear as to each character's UA.

In the case of the wartime spy, Captain Desmond Johnson, his ultimate aim might be: 'To overcome his amnesia and prevent his enemies from winning the war.' His impediment is his amnesia. Although this UA covers everything, it does sound a little vague, simply because we haven't worked out what the entire story is yet. That's fine. You shouldn't hold up constructing your outline simply because you've not managed to place every piece of the jigsaw. You'll be surprised how easily your story falls into place as you move through the outlining process in sequence.

Once you have worked in an impediment for your main character, deciding on their ultimate aim is usually pretty straightforward. It's to overcome whatever the impediment is and…

- Rescue the kidnapped wife or daughter and restore life to how it was before the kidnapping;
- To win the war and return home safely;
- To return the ring to its rightful home and prevent the forces of evil from destroying the Shires…

…and so on

Very often the aim in most (though not all) cases is to return life to how it was before the 'terrible thing' happened. The 'terrible thing' is what story gurus call the *Inciting Incident*. That's the event that kicks off the story: the alien invasion, the earthquake, the kidnapping of the daughter, the first murder, the diagnosis of terminal illness, or whatever.

When a character's circumstances are pretty bad at the start of the story, such as when the lead character is a slave in the American Deep South or a prisoner on death row, the aim would be to enjoy a better future away from slavery or penal confinement.

What Motivates The Antagonist Will Decide Their Ultimate Aim

The UA of an antagonist can be harder to pin down. In the case of The Stripper, for example, has he an end-game already decided, or is he on a killing spree until he is stopped or drops dead of old age? That's something you've got to decide before you can produce that character's UA. You don't have to work out an impediment for anyone other than the lead character, but you do need to decide on what motivates the villain.

This highlights one of the great strengths of this method of outlining. In far too many novels and movies, the reader never really gets to find out why the bad guys do what they do. What is it that drives them to become serial killers, or gangsters, or drug dealers, in the first place? All too often, we are supposed to assume they were born evil, or that some kind of mental illness has turned them bad.

To satisfy your readers, you have to convince them your characters are 'real'. This is even more relevant when it comes to the antagonist.

This isn't as hard as it sounds. When a reader opens a new novel they are expecting to be entertained. They've already decided your novel looks like 'their kind of thing' and they have high hopes for your story. They really want to believe in your characters. All you have to do is give them a vaguely plausible scenario they can live with.

The BBC drama series, *McMafia*, worked well partly because it blurred the areas of grey between the heroes and the villains. None of the bad guys were truly very bad and none of the good guys were really very good. The Russian gangster, Vadim, calls off the assassination attempt on the 'hero' because he's having such a great time at his daughter's school event. He lives to regret his decision, but that's not the point.

The easiest way to work out an antagonist's UA is usually to start by deciding what it is that motivates them. One of the strengths of *The Godfather* is how the depictions of poverty and oppression in Don Corleone's early life, coupled with the traditions of his Sicilian background, led him into the Mafia. I'm not suggesting you go into such drawn-out detail in your novel, just that you think about motivation, and how you can communicate your conclusions to the reader.

It is pretty much accepted that some bad guys are motivated by greed and the desire for easy money. This is the case with most heist and kidnap thrillers. It doesn't explain the classic scenario of two friends being brought up in the same childhood circumstances, where one turns to crime and the other becomes a cop. Maybe this is to do with genes, or perhaps the attitude of parents or guardians? A chance bad (or good) experience in childhood? Who knows.

I don't think it's a great idea to leave the motivation unsaid or vague, especially as the fix is so easy. As the creator of the story, it's up to you to decide what motivates every character, and to communicate this information to the readers.

What is the catalyst that turns a loyal employee into the mastermind of an inside job robbery? Being passed over for promotion, or needing money because his wife has been diagnosed with cancer, are just two possible reasons that have been done almost to death.

What might transform a patriotic American into a spy for a foreign nation? Why would a loyal and faithful wife seek the attentions of a younger man? Why did Jack the Ripper murder seemingly random women so mercilessly in Victorian London?

Work out a plausible reason for why the antagonist is opposing your hero and make it part of the story. My advice would be to keep it as simple as possible. The reader only wants to 'tick a box' not take a degree course in advanced psychology.

Ultimate Aims Of Key Secondary Characters

Although I don't advocate you pinpoint the UA of every single character in your story, being aware of the ultimate aims of key secondary characters can be useful when you are constructing the outline. It makes it easier to plot and to keep your story consistent.

If one of the junior detectives working on a police case is corrupt, their UA becomes, 'to make money by derailing the investigation and ensuring the antagonists escape arrest.' If your hero encounters a Troll King on his quest for the Holy Grail who's UA is to 'destroy the human race so that Trolls can rule the Underworld,' then you need to know that before you start writing those chapters.

I try and work out UAs for every character I think might have a pivotal role in the story. Of course, I add to and amend these as I continue the outlining process.

Character Progression

IN REAL LIFE, people are affected by their environment and by what happens to them. We've all read novels and seen movies containing 'cardboard characters'. Nothing seems to affect them. They are exactly the same on the last page as they were on page one. This is bad writing.

It's also unnecessary. As in life, fictional characters must be seen to change because of what they've been through. I like to call it 'character progression' which, to my mind, is more illustrative than the standard term, 'character arc.' It doesn't take more than a few minutes to add life to your characters by thinking how their attitudes might change during the course of the story and acting on it.

A meek, mild-mannered librarian who is forced to escape from terrorists and jump out of a burning building is a good example. Most of us aren't built to climb down ropes into 500 feet lift shafts, but if your life depends on it, I'm pretty sure you'd like to think you'd just grit your teeth and get on with it. Those who can't tend to be the ones who end up plummeting to their deaths in disaster movies.

If the librarian is fundamentally the same person at the end of the novel as she is at the beginning, the audience will be disappointed and the author will have failed. Character progression is important.

I use the word 'progression' because characters don't always get better or more exciting during the course of the story. They can have breakdowns, become ill, or deteriorate. They can become bitter and spiteful. The mugging victim may withdraw from society and become a paranoid recluse.

The best way for an author to begin mapping character progression is to reflect on how that person is before the story opens, before the Inciting Incident. Then imagine how they would be at the end of the story. In between, a lot's going to happen to most of your characters. How do they react to each twist and turn in your story? Don't worry, you don't have to be 100% accurate 100% of the time: after all, it's only a story.

Character arc implies a gradual change from chapter one to the end of your story, which simply wouldn't happen. Let's look at *The Fugitive* movie.

When Dr Richard Kimble discovers the one-armed man has murdered his wife, he attempts to fight him but loses. At this stage, he is still a normal MD, who can't summon up the adrenalin or strength to overcome a man with one arm. This Kimble is a regular guy who believes in justice, and who thinks the authorities can be trusted to seek out the villain who really killed his wife. But once he is suspected by the police and unjustly convicted of her murder, he is forced to change his ideas.

By the time he escapes from the prison bus transporting him to death row, Kimble has become a man desperate enough to fight for his life. He has become aware he is the only person with enough motivation to bring the one-armed man to justice. Would the MD at the beginning of the movie have dared to jump into the raging waters of the dam to escape Deputy US Marshal Sam Gerard? You bet he wouldn't. By this point, Kimble has already gone through enormous change, and the movie's only a quarter way in.

Kimble's leap into the dam will have changed him and the way he thinks. Although it was born out of desperation and the desire not to get caught, its success must have filled him with confidence. If he can do something like that, surely he's capable of anything? Every event and close shave that follows alters Kimble's character. The process is not so much an 'arc,' more a zig-zagged graph with enormous spikes early on in the story.

You will probably already have an idea how your story will end, so it's possible now to write down a rough summary of your lead character's progression from who he or she was at the start of the novel, to how they are at the end. Something like this:

- *Character Progression*: Steve Simpson begins the story as a seemingly confident detective, but he has crippling self-doubt, and secretly suffers panic attacks. Because of this, he appears arrogant and a loner. By the end of the novel, he has become more self-confident and a better team player, though not entirely cured. He does still suffer the occasional panic attack but does his best to keep it to himself.

It's clunky, I know, but no one else is going to see it, and there's no point in holding up the outlying process to try and make it perfect. I can come back and improve it later if that's what I *really* want to do.

A quick note about endings: Don't be afraid to change the ending of your story once you've begun writing if you feel you need to or if something more original occurs to you. Sometimes you'll get great ideas during the writing process, based on what you're learning about your characters and about the story. As I say, nothing in an outline is written in stone.

The Premise

THE *PREMISE* or *theme* is the statement that sums up a novel or screenplay's core idea in a single sentence or phrase. Sadly, it's not as straightforward as you'd expect. Different people regard the premise in different ways.

When I was conducting research, the more books I read and the more experts I consulted, the more confused I became. You'd never think they were all talking about the same thing — and very often they weren't. The premise taught by John Truby is a very different beast to that of Robert McKee. Another renowned exponent, James N Frey, has a different idea again, and so it goes on.

I once attended a creative fiction writing course where we were shown how to construct a premise and most of them ended up sounding like Ancient Greek fables. Take the example of *The Three Little Pigs*. Somewhat surprisingly (to me, at least), the premise is not 'a wolf can only be kept at bay by brick houses,' but something along the lines of: 'Stupidity will end in disaster, just as good sense leads to happiness.'

Screenwriting guru Robert McKee doesn't spend much time talking about the premise. To him, it's not really that important. "A premise is not precious," he writes in *Story*.

"As long as it contributes to the growth of the story, keep it, but should the telling take a left turn, abandon the original inspiration to follow the evolving story."

John Truby, on the other hand, teaches that premise is one of the most important aspects of a story and must be adhered to at all times. His view is that if you feel the need to stray outside it, you have the wrong premise.

In *Anatomy of Story*, Truby says: "A premise is your story stated in one sentence." He then goes on to detail a ten-step method of creating a premise that will be "so crucial to your success."

My own view falls somewhere in-between that of McKee and Truby. I build a premise to make my story better. If it isn't going to achieve that modest result, what's the point? On the other hand, I don't want to spend too long working it out.

A useful premise will fulfil two roles:

- To define the core aspect of the story; and,
- Provide reference points that will prevent me from straying off track.

It's certainly possible to write successfully without one but why make the job harder? My own method of building one does practically the same job as John Truby's only without the hard slog.

My Three-Step Method To Creating A Workable Premise

The premise should not be so much about plot as about consequences. We need to look at the story's beginning and at its ending and see what happens to the central character in between.

It may be possible to construct a premise without knowing exactly how a story will pan out but, to make it work efficiently, we need to know three things:

- The **Beginning** of the story.
- The **Conclusion**.
- Who the **Lead Character** is and how he/she will progress from *Beginning* to *Conclusion*.

To discover exactly what I need to know, I ask myself three questions:

1. How does the story end?
2. How did the lead character achieve this?
3. What was the situation at the start of the story?

You don't have to stick religiously to this order, and I recommend you answer questions whichever way you find easiest. In my case, I do it in the order that seems most natural for the circumstances of the story. It's usually different every time.

The premise I'm looking for will describe what happens to the protagonist from chapter one to the climax of the story. That's why those three questions are so valuable.

The next step is to study the answers —making adjustments, if necessary, for the sake of coherence and clarity — to construct a single-sentence premise.

Let's look at an example. I'll start with the classic movie, *Casablanca*, which I guess most people are familiar with. If I was building a premise for *Casablanca*, it would be something like: 'A world-weary American expatriate reunites by chance with a former lover but in the end he does the decent thing and gives her up to her husband to go and fight the Nazis.'

It may not be very pretty, but it works. Your sentence will probably be rambling and it doesn't have to sound as if it was written by a great writer. You will be the only person who ever reads it, so prettiness shouldn't be a big factor.

What would the answer to the three questions be in the case of *Casablanca*? Let's try it and find out:

1. How does the story end? *When Renault (Police Chief) tries to arrest Laszlo, Rick forces him to help them escape. Rick makes Ilsa board the plane to Lisbon with Laszlo, telling her that she would regret it if she stayed: "Maybe not today, maybe not tomorrow, but soon and for the rest of your life."*

2. How did the lead character achieve this? *(This is where we need to use our head). To help Laszlo in his efforts to defeat the Nazis, Rick sacrificed his chance of being with Ilsa by orchestrating their escape.*

3. How did the story begin? *In December 1941, American expatriate Rick Blaine owns an upscale nightclub and gambling den in Casablanca. "Rick's Café Américain" attracts a varied clientele, including Vichy French and German officials, refugees desperate to reach the still-neutral United States, and those who prey on them.*

The *Casablanca* premise works because it defines the central character, Rick, who begins the story saying one thing (that he only cares about looking after number one) and ends up taking a heroic stance for the good of others. Along the way, we see how he changes and why. In effect Rick has returned to how he was at a time before the film started. As we see in flashback, he only became bitter and cynical after he thought Ilsa had abandoned him.

Let's take another example from cinema. A premise that seems to work for *Three Billboards Outside Ebbing Missouri*: 'A disillusioned bereaved mother takes action to stir up the police investigation on behalf of her murdered daughter and finds common ground with an officer she thought was against her.' I say "seems to work" because I stress we are creating a 'premise' after seeing the completed film. I'd bet writer/director/producer Martin McDonagh worked with something quite different when he first came to plot the movie.

To construct a premise for our example Detective story in which Inspector Stephanie (Stevie) Simpson battles the serial killer, I'd start by asking myself a variation of the three questions.

The first question: 'How does the story end?' *Inspector Stevie Simpson catches The Stripper and so safeguards her family.*

The next question: 'How does she do it?' *By careful police work and by overcoming her own self-doubts.*

Finally, 'How does the story begin?' *Detective Chief Inspector Stephanie 'Stevie' Simpson is a competent police officer but secretly full of self-doubt, which she is unable to overcome.*

So… I'd write down a sentence. (Remember, at this stage I'm still fishing.) I'd say, 'hard work, dedication, and love, can overcome evil and self-doubt.'

There, it's done.

I don't think it's a perfectly-worded premise, but I'll go along with it, at least for now.

Character Biographies

SOME WRITERS really go to town getting to know their characters. They write 50+ page biographies for each of them, conduct interviews, and who knows what else. Part of the reason they have to do it is because they don't have the information we've already compiled as Ultimate Aims and Character Progression. That's valuable data that will help you know the people inhabiting your novel and puts you way ahead of the field.

I suggest you write fairly detailed biographies for both your protagonist and your antagonist: the hero and the villain. Not as many as 50 pages, but I personally like to write something between 500-1,500 words, depending on how much there is to say.

As ever in this process, don't use the numbers I'm quoting as targets: the figures are only meant as rough guides. Just write as much as you need to and then stop. You'll probably add more when you come to write the outline itself. If the word-count approaches 5,000 words, don't beat yourself up. Similarly, if you can only think of 500 relevant words, don't be tempted to waffle or add stuff for the sake of it.

Don't feel you have to share every detail in the biography

with your reader. These biographies exist entirely for your own benefit and might contain information you won't get around to using until book 3 or even book 30 in a series — if at all.

The main functions are to prevent inconsistencies creeping into your stories and to help you work out what makes each character tick.

If I had to write The Stripper's biography, it would look something like this:

'The Stripper,' real name Ronald Morgan, a barrister working out of Gray's Inn, in central London. He is 58 years old and comes from a small village in South Wales called Foelgastell. When alive, his father was the local solicitor and a very devout Methodist. Ronald's much-loved mother died when he was seven and he was sent away to boarding school. When he returned, he found his father had taken a new wife, a frightening woman who wore too much makeup called Megan. She used to get secretly drunk and bully him.

Ronald was never good with women, and after many years in all-male boarding schools, he left home forever to go away to university in Cardiff to study law. He never fitted in or was able to mix with the other students, who nicknamed him the 'Undertaker'. Curiosity took him to a strip club in London, where the women he saw on stage reminded him of his stepmother, and he fled, terrified and dissatisfied.

After gaining his degree, Ronald was able to secure a place to train as a barrister at Gray's Inn. In an attempt to fit in, he asks his landlady's daughter out on a date, which didn't go well. Afterward, he overhears her talking to her parents about him, ridiculing him and being unkind. He vowed never to go on another date with a woman ever again.

Thirty years later, Ronald relents. He has become quite well-off and successful in the intervening years and lives alone in a large flat on Bloomsbury Square. He has become intrigued by a middle-aged neighbour, Alice Friend (44). They pass in the hallways and occasionally make small talk. He eventually summons up the courage to ask her out on a date. Both of them are lonely and, after one or two meals out, she invites him back to her apartment for a meal.

Despite her staid appearance, Alice has been sexually active. After the two of them consume a little too much wine, she strips off her clothes and attempts to engage Ronald in oral sex. He is horrified and tries to get her to stop. Mistaking his reaction for role-playing, she intensifies her assault and he strangles her, almost without meaning to. Afterward, he is both horrified and elated at being a murderer.

Using his legal knowledge, Ronald makes it look as though someone has broken into Alice's flat, then leaves. He engineers a foolproof alibi for himself (NOTE: how????). The police interview him, but he is able to persuade them he had left the apartment before the murder took place. Ronald is an upstanding member of the community with a clean record, they cannot find any evidence against him, and so he is eliminated from the enquiry.

Ronald finds he enjoyed the excitement of the kill and endeavours to arrange a 'proper murder' as an experiment. He finds he likes that, too, and so begins his alternate career as a serial killer.

You'll notice that the biography contains quite a lot of plot detail that can be used in the novel. At this stage, I'd be tempted to at least begin the novel from Ronald's point of view. When I'd bring Stevie Simpson into the story and establish her as the lead character, is a matter I'd have to think about at the outlining stage. The story could end up as a battle of wits between the two of them.

Minor And Recurring Characters

How many characters you write biographies for is entirely up to you. Certainly, the two main characters need to be covered in some detail, everyone else, far less. I usually write short biographies for characters who are in any way connected to the story or who will potentially be returning in some way. I say, 'potentially' because you never know until the outline is completed who will end up doing what. Plus there will undoubtedly be more novels to come in this 'bestselling' series!

When I'm writing up minor characters, the upper limit for me is around 500 words, but most get far fewer. Don't try and write *War and Peace*: you need just enough information to prevent mistakes being made. *Age, nationality, appearance, foibles*, that kind of thing.

Keep Up To Date

When you come to write the detailed outline (and indeed the novel itself), you've got to be careful you don't add a detail such as height or something the character reveals in conversation that's not in the biography. If that crops up, it is essential you come back and add it. Nothing labels a writer as more amateurish than a character who is described as short on page 13, bangs his head on the top of a door frame on page 67, and is dismissed as 'of average height,' on page 155.

I must confess, I like to write words for every character that appears in the novel. Most of them only occupy a line of text: name, age, and brief description of their role. Something like this:

Jasper Godchild (76). White-haired old retainer who lives

alone in Cadby Hall and keeps it in order. Walks with a stoop.

If nothing else, it prevents me from forgetting his name and from using something similar (such as Jason Goodbody) that would confuse the reader.

Don't Name Characters Unless You Have To

One really useful tip I picked up relatively recently is not to name characters that don't need future identification. If you give a name to every single person who appears in your book, pretty soon the reader will be overloaded with irrelevant identities they think think they have to remember.

The leader of the inter-galactic space corps who ambushes your hero can be identified as 'the corps leader', or maybe use his (or her) rank. *The captain did this, the sergeant did that*, and so on.

The three police officers who accompany Chief Inspector Simpson to search the suspect's mansion don't need names unless you're going to give one (or all) of them a future role in the story. You could say, 'one searched in the kitchen, another in the bathroom, and the third joined Stevie in the cellar.

Minor characters who appear once and have no role in how the story plays out can be 'a tall cowboy, with stained blue suede shoes,' or just 'the waiter read out the menu and took everyone's order'. We do not need to know that the cowboy's name is Wayne Dexter III or that he comes from Amarillo.

Putting It All Together

IT'S TIME TO RECAP. Here's that list again:

1. Who Is It For?
2. Overview
3. Ultimate Aims
4. Character Progression
5. The Premise
6. Character Outlines

We need to make sure we have the information assembled and ready to go. In the case of our Detective story with DCI Stevie Simpson and The Stripper, it might look something like this:

1. *Who Is It For?* Our ideal reader is Mary. She is approximately 50 years old and lives in the American Midwest. She enjoys novels by Ian Rankin, Michael Connelly, Lee Child, and David Baldacci.
2. *Overview:* A serial killer called The Stripper is on the loose in southeast London, preying on attractive

young women who live alone. He traps them in their apartment, strangles them, before removing their clothes, and laying them out in poses reminiscent of strippers.

Leading the Murder Squad assigned to investigating The Stripper is Detective Chief Inspector Stephanie 'Stevie' Simpson, who is 42 years old, and lives in Blackheath with husband, Carl (39), and daughter Abigail (14). Due to bullying at school, Stevie lacks self-belief and frequently suffers from panic attacks. So far, she has managed to keep this from her colleagues in the police.

Stevie's boss is Superintendent Alan Wise (53), and they are based at Lewisham Police Station. Stevie's number two in her squad is Detective Sergeant Jaspreet Gill (36), an ambitious career detective, and Detective Constable Colin Dexter (26), a thorough but less-than-inspiring detective who does everything by the book. Although they seldom put their thoughts into words, Wise and members of his team are silently resentful that Stevie is a poor delegator who prefers to work alone.

There is an indication that the killer is receiving inside information about the investigation, which points to a 'mole' inside the police. Thanks to a tip-off (NOTE: how did that come about???), Stevie almost catches The Stripper in action, but he escapes and threatens to attack and kill Stevie's husband and daughter unless she backs off. The Stripper has already shown he kills without remorse and with impunity. Does Stevie tell anyone about the threats and so risk her family's life, or does she work alone to catch the murderer?

---

1. *Ultimate Aims:* <u>DCI Stevie Simpson</u>: To overcome

her crippling self-doubt and bring The Stripper to justice to ensure the safety of her husband and daughter.

2. *Character Progression:* <u>Stevie Simpson</u> begins the story as a seemingly confident detective but, underneath her protective shell, she has crippling self-doubt, and secretly suffers panic attacks. Because of this, she appears arrogant and a loner. By the end of the novel, Stevie has become more self-confident and a better team player, though not entirely cured. She does still suffer the occasional panic attack.

3. *The Premise:* Hard work, dedication, and love, can overcome evil and self-doubt.

We covered biographies in the last section, which means we are almost good to go. But, before we can get started, there are things we need to know about the craft of storytelling to make it all work smoothly. That's what the next chapter is all about.

Plotline

WE'LL HAVE to go back over some of what we've already learned in previous chapters. If you find this annoying, please feel free to stick pins into a doll shaped in my likeness, but I think it's important I make everything as clear as possible.

You'll remember way back at the start, I shared with you a particularly gruesome story template I found online. To save your memory, this was it:

ACT ONE

1. The Ordinary World
2. Inciting Incident
3. The Call To Adventure
4. The Lock In

ACT TWO

1. Tests & Trials
2. First Failure
3. The Midpoint
4. Major Setback

5. All Hope Is Lost

ACT THREE

1. Inspiring Incident
2. Girding The Loins
3. Climax (Final Battle)
4. Stinger

Writers use 'plotting aids' like this because stories do need a certain amount of structure. Don't let that worry you. I'd never be so cruel as to ask you to conform to such rigidity. What we are going to do is look at how a story can be structured and see what we can learn from it.

This is where I remind you about the traditional three-act structure:

Act 1: Beginning
Act 2: Middle
Act 3: End

As you already know, the middle act is usually twice as long as the other two, making it around half the size of the entire novel. So far, so good…

I must stress at this stage that you don't have to follow this framework slavishly but I find it useful when I start to work out a plot line. I can — and usually do – go off-piste after the initial flurry.

Act One/Inciting Incident/Lock Down

Every story I can think of contains an event early on that disturbs the status quo. This is called the *Inciting Incident* and it signals the end of Act One by forcing the protagonist to take action. This is where the vicar is murdered, the daughter is kidnapped, the first tremor of the earthquake is detected. It is the event that begins the process that leads to the story's conclusion.

The Inciting Incident is usually, though not always, something bad. In the story, the aim of the lead character is generally to return life to how it was before the event took place. The murderer is caught and sent to jail; the daughter is returned to her family and the culprit punished; the restoration of the town begins and the inhabitants start to rebuild their lives.

You'll notice that it's not enough just for the murders to stop or for the daughter to be returned to the family. The threat has to be removed in order for it to be considered a satisfactory conclusion. In the case of the earthquake, there's not a lot that can be done to stop it happening again, and we can only console ourselves with the notion that Acts of God are relatively rare.

The Inciting Incident must be something truly overwhelming. A murder, a kidnapping or, in the case of a Romance, something major like an earth-shattering meeting. Having your lead character fall over and twist his or her ankle might not cut it. For your novel to succeed, the stakes have to be high and the Inciting Incident is the event that begins the process.

Traditionally, the very first part of a story will show the reader what everyday life is like before things went wrong. This might be achieved by showing the family having Saturday morning breakfast together; the town going about its normal business; the victim very much alive and likeable, enjoying a night out with friends, and so on. You get the idea…

Get this right and you've already started to formulate a structure for your novel. *Painless, wasn't it?*

The next step is to bring in our lead character: the hero or heroine. It's quite possible we've already seen them in the opening section — the father at breakfast, the Sheriff joking with townsfolk — but not always. There are plenty of ways to go on this and we don't want to tie ourselves down to following clichés.

The hero or heroine (let's say the name's Joe) has to be committed to tackling the problem the Inciting Incident brings up. If Joe is not a cop or a firefighter, just an ordinary citizen, you have to show a good reason why he's taking action and not leaving it to the authorities. Again, that's up to you to decide and demonstrate.

Next, we have to make sure Joe will stick it out for the duration of the novel. To do this, we have to introduce something writing coaches call the 'Point of No Return' or 'Lock Down'. If Joe decides things are getting too dangerous or maybe it's just harder than he thought, we can't allow him to give up, otherwise our entire story crumbles.

Of course, if Joe is a cop he can still resign, retire, or get killed, and pass the baton on to another Joe. That is your choice and, handled correctly, it can be an interesting plot twist. Just make sure the reader already cares about what happens to the replacement Joe.

Ideally, we need the first Joe to stay on track. There are a wide variety of ways this can be achieved. In the case of having his daughter kidnapped, we don't need to think about it too much. What father would walk away when his little girl was in danger? Maybe you could crank up his motivation by having the kidnappers give Joe a ransom demand containing some kind of deadline?

If Joe was the town Sheriff and all his friends (and voters) needed rescuing from the effects of the earthquake, that would be motivation enough. He'd be a pretty poor type of guy if he gave up and went on vacation. The police detective is another professional. Even if she or he did give up, someone else would soon step into their shoes.

Act One ends with the Lock Down, Gateway, or maybe

even The Doorway of No Return (a more extreme type of Lock Down). TDoNR is most often used in Science Fiction, Fantasy, and Horror stories. The Gateway is the one-way door that prevents the protagonist from returning to their normal, everyday life, and it is also what forces them into action.

Of course, it helps build the tension if the reader thinks life can never return to normal following the Inciting Incident. This will literally be the case in post-Apocalyptic stories, in which case, the best that can be hoped for is a happy, threat-free existence.

To create a Gateway that achieves the vital 'one-way' element, the writer needs to pretty much blow away the status quo. The protagonist must have no other option than to take action. In *Gone With The Wind*, this is achieved by the outbreak of the Civil War. In the original *Star Wars* movie, the same point is reached when Luke returns home to find that imperial stormtroopers have killed his aunt and uncle and destroyed their moisture farm.

Neither Scarlett O'Hara nor Luke Skywalker have any say in the events that forced them into action, nor can they reverse them. The American Civil War has begun and the clock cannot be turned back. Luke does not have the power to reincarnate his aunt and uncle. His only way forward is to join the rebellion.

Act Two/Midpoint

We're now in Act Two, which is where most of the novel's action takes place. If we were following the goofy template I showed you, we'd now be worrying about stuff like Tests & Trials and First Failure. But we're not, so don't concern yourself.

You will notice that we have followed the template pretty much up to this point. This is not proof that the template is so brilliant, it's just that what we've done is the obvious way to go and the only way that's simple and really works. From now on, we're on our own.

Although we're not worrying about Tests & Trials and First Failures, we have to get Joe working on solving his problem. This is where your knowledge of the genre you are writing in comes into play. If it were a detective story, Joe would be going to autopsies and following up on clues. In a fantasy, he might be starting on a quest or visiting someone that can give him special weapons or some such.

This is where your imagination is so important. Joe has to do his best to get to where he wants to be, to reach his ultimate aim. It's going to be hard for him because his opposition is better than he is. It has to be, or the story will be weak and uninteresting.

If you've ever attended any kind of creative writing course, you will have heard the word 'conflict'. That's what this is: conflict between Joe and those who are opposing him.

Conflict! Conflict! Conflict!

Joe has to be up against a worthy opponent or trying to solve an impossible puzzle. He has to appear way out of his depth. Nothing worthwhile happens without conflict, whether we are talking about external conflict (a puzzle, whodunnit, or villain), or internal conflict (self-doubt, drink or drug problem, etc).

To achieve the best effect, the conflict must build up to a climax. You can't start with a bang and then wimp out. To keep the reader's attention, it is important you generate a momentum that drives your story towards its conclusion. When Indiana Jones goes up against Arab warriors, the first fight isn't against a hundred men on horses, then three men with swords, then one man and a stick. Things have to get harder, not easier.

Throw in a few surprises. Try not to write by numbers. Rather than say, 'Joe attends the autopsy where the medical officer extracts the bullet which is matched to the same gun that…' throw in a surprise. Have him find a 100-year-old postage stamp rolled up inside the victim's nose. You'll obviously have to work out how that fits into your plot, but that's the fun part.

Work very hard not to be predictable. Instead of saying, 'This happens, then this happens, and then this…' throw in a few cases of 'supposing he does this instead,' and 'what would happen if?'. Remember to run everything by your target reader (at least in your head).

The Midpoint

At roughly halfway through your novel — and by extension, midway through Act Two — you might want to insert a Midpoint scene.

The Midpoint can be a major plot twist or it can simply be the scene in which the protagonist hits rock bottom and things can't seem to get any worse. It's not absolutely essential: some novels and screenplays don't bother with a Midpoint scene at all. I personally like to have one because it helps give the second act a better structure and prevents it from getting boring and repetitive.

In a thriller, the Midpoint could be where we discover the identity of the villain. Or, maybe the reader learns that the guy the hero thinks is his best friend has actually been working for the opposition all along.

It's not essential that any of the characters share the knowledge that's revealed to the readers. It can even be information the characters knew all along — for instance, that the protagonist murdered his father as a child — but it's the first time the reader is hearing about it. The Midpoint exists purely for the readers' benefit.

If you're going for a big surprise, my advice is to not to make it too surprising. You must plant some seeds leading up to the reveal. For example, if a sweet old lady is shown to be a vampire and there's nothing in the preceding chapters suggesting she might be, readers will feel cheated. On the other hand, if they can think back and pick up on the subtle clues you've dropped, they are more likely to praise your storytelling skills.

Moving Into Act Three/The Second Gateway

At the end of Act 2, Joe still hasn't succeeded. Maybe he's had a small victory, that's up to you. Maybe he thinks he's succeeded, only to be proved wrong. Again, it's your choice. My advice is to make your story as fresh and interesting as you can, remembering you have another important act coming up.

Usually it's a good idea to have Joe want to throw in the towel at some point. If or when you decide to do this is entirely up to you, though it will look silly if it's too early in the story. I advise you not to drag it on for too long. One or two scenes is usually enough before something or someone persuades him to carry on.

Whatever happens, it has to look like the opposition is bound to succeed in the end. They are so very powerful... The case the detective is working on is so difficult to solve... The puzzle the professor must figure out is so insoluble... The reader probably knows that's not going to be the case, but you have to use every weapon in your arsenal to try and convince them they're wrong.

You need a major event at the end of Act 2. It's entirely your choice what it is, but it really has to be something significant. Maybe Joe's closest friend is killed or is shown to be on the side of the opposition. Perhaps Joe is arrested for something he didn't do. There's a terrible battle that ends in defeat. The opposition is shown to be much stronger than Joe thought... whatever.

Be Creative.

We are moving towards the 'Second Gateway'. This will force the protagonist to up his or her game. Often, this can be another 'doorway of no return.' Maybe your main character is on the verge of losing everything and the only way to possibly get it back is to go 'all in'.

Act Three

We're now moving into the third and final act. This is where the story must be resolved, one way or another. There's no need for you to return everything to how it was before the Inciting Incident, but if it's possible to do so, and you don't, your readers will not like it.

I sometimes like to give Joe a boost quite early on in Act Three, but I never overdo it. I'm a fan of the false ending, but it's not something you can use every time. Maybe Joe sets a trap and a suspect falls into it: general jubilation! The bad guy is caught, only it turns out not to be the serial killer he's been searching for. Something like that.

You've no doubt heard the expression, *It's always darkest just before the dawn*. You can choose to take advantage of it in your novel, or you can go straight to the climax. This is a big moment for you and for Joe.

The climax has to be just that and *not* an anti-climax. Save your best for last.

Perceived wisdom suggests that writers should lavish the most attention on opening lines and on the first chapter. Although these are undoubtedly important areas of your novel, I always try and spend as much — if not more — time making sure the ending is as good as I can possibly make it. After all, as the ultimate commercial novelist, Micky Spillane, used to say, "The first chapter sells the book; the last chapter sells the next book."

Never forget that your reader is wanting you to surprise them. That's the case, no matter what genre you are working in, except possibly when it comes to Romance. It's invariably best to do what your readers want; otherwise, you'll be letting them down. That's *never* a good idea for a commercial novelist, believe me.

There are only five possible ways to end any story:

- **The Positive ending**. Joe wins and the opposition is sent packing. This is the one you'll come across most often in commercial fiction and in cinema.
- **Negative ending**. Joe is defeated and the bad guy wins. Wouldn't be very popular with readers unless you managed to pull off some kind of brilliant writing trick!
- **Ambiguous positive ending**. This is a good one. Joe fails to achieve his Ultimate Aim, but everything works out all right anyway. Maybe, unknown to Joe, the serial killer was involved in a traffic accident and is languishing in a coma in some out of the way hospital. A good ending, because it means Joe's goal is achieved almost by proxy, plus it leaves things open for possible sequels.
- **Ambiguous negative ending**. Joe gets what he strives for, but it turns out not to be what he wanted after all. In *Murder On The Orient Express*, Agatha Christie has Poirot discover the murderers' identity but he decides not to close the case and notify the authorities because he agrees that the victim 'deserved to die'. Or, maybe Joe was a cattle rancher who was desperate to keep the sheep farmers out of Kansas. He fails, but only because he falls in love with a sheepman's daughter and realises they're not so bad after all.

- **Non-ending**. The novel or movie just ends without any resolution. Hard to justify unless you die before you finish writing it. I can't find a single example of a well-reviewed novel with a non-ending, so I suggest you don't even consider it. At least not until you've made your first couple of million.

Aim For An Explosive Ending

Don't try and rush through the final act. What happens immediately before the final resolution has to be just as good as you can make it. Work on it. If necessary, hold back ideas from Act Two to use in the climax.

Believe me, everyone who reads your novel will be looking for an explosive ending. If you don't deliver, they'll be disappointed, no matter how good the rest of the story is. Acts one and two should build up to the climax, which needs to go off like 100 tons of dynamite. Avoid the damp squib at all costs!

Because we are outlining before we sit down to write the novel, we can go back and add or change events in earlier parts of the story to signal what's going to happen. We definitely do not want the reader to be able to predict the ending at any point in the novel but an 'aha' moment at the end is certainly worth striving for.

As I've said before, by choosing to read your novel in the first place, the reader has given you permission to mislead and surprise them (in a good way). They'll be disappointed if you don't.

Once The Dust Starts To Settle...

My advice is to work out as many possible endings as you can. Make a list. Include every conceivable ending you can think of, even ones that seem ridiculous and totally implausible. When you're pretty sure you can't think of any more, stop and take a look at what you've written.

Find the most likely ending. The one you'd expect to read in a novel you'd bought in the bookstore or see on TV. Cross it out.

Take another look and try and find the ending that would surprise you if you read it in someone else's novel. One you'd not expected. Be sure it makes perfect sense. If not, you'll be shooting yourself in the foot.

By the time the novel is done and dusted, you've got to make sure you've tied up every loose end. The reader should be left looking forward to getting hold of your next story, not wondering who the man with the yellow waistcoat in chapter twenty-three worked for.

Creating The Outline

Putting Theory Into Practice

HAVING READ THIS FAR, you've got all the information you need to start working on your novel's outline. Now it's mostly a question of applying the techniques.

The way I produce outlines is pretty similar to the methods used by James Patterson and Ken Follett. The biggest difference — especially in the case of Mr Patterson — is that I don't spend weeks and weeks honing it down and producing draft after draft. It's hard to say how many drafts I go through, largely because I edit as I go along. So, I suppose that means I create a single draft with lots of corrections.

From now on, I'll put aside the examples we've been working on. Otherwise, we're in danger of becoming too specific and obscuring the overall view.

The material we've already produced for our story is vitally important.

1. Who's It For?
2. Overview
3. Ultimate Aims
4. Character Progressions
5. The Premise

6. Character Biographies

Everything that's already been decided is the basis of what we are going to write. Every event we include in the outline has to tie in with what's written here. If we make fundamental changes to anything, we have to change it here first. That way we keep the novel consistent and on track.

Once the Premise is decided on and we start writing, every scene we write must be compatible with the thrust of the Premise, or it doesn't go in. If we ignore this rule, we risk allowing the story to go off-track and become flabby. If you are forced to change the Premise of your story for whatever reason, it's important to go back and make sure what you've already done ties in with the new structure. If not, edit or cut it. You have to be ruthless.

There's another strict rule:

Every scene you write has to advance the story in some way, or you cut it.

I've given that rule a line by itself and made it bold. That's how important it is. Your novel is the story, that's all it should be. It's totally fine to have sub-plots, provided they have some relation to the main thrust of the novel. If the lead character's child is struggling with depression or is taking difficult exams, it can only add human interest and put extra pressure on the poor protagonist. That's a sub-plot that actually adds weight to the main story.

You'll remember in old TV cop shows like *Cagney and Lacey*, *Miami Vice* and *The Rockford Files*, where there'd be subplots about a character's cousin coming in from out of town, a kid being bullied at school, or someone's wife or husband having a health scare. These strands of sub-plot wouldn't just appear out of nowhere, there'd be a reason for having them. It's called *good writing*.

It's not OK to go off on some flight of fancy that has nothing to do with the main story. I can guarantee that your mind will do its best to sidetrack you, and try and convince you that what you've written is the best work you've ever done, but ignore it. Stick to the narrative.

Remember to consider your target reader whenever you make a decision about plot or story. Although I'll be the first to admit it's not a particularly scientific way to go about things, it does force you to think about your potential audience. I'm sure it will help stop you from losing them along the way.

Write A Summary

At this point, I find it useful to write a Summary of what I've already got. It's a file I refer back to and update as I come to write the final outline. It's important to keep it up to date as you work on your story. Although the Summary is primarily for my own use, it often proves itself useful and will form the basis of a blurb or any overview of the story I might have to write.

I write the Summary in one long flowing narrative. It's like I'm explaining the story to someone who has no idea who any of the characters or locations are. This forces me to make the story entertaining and logical. Something like this Wikipedia plot summary of the 1939 Agatha Christie novel, *Murder Is Easy* (aka *Easy To Kill*):

Luke Fitzwilliam happens to share a London-bound train carriage with Lavinia Pinkerton, an elderly lady who informs Luke that she is travelling to Scotland Yard to report a serial killer, responsible for the deaths of three people: Amy Gibbs, Tommy Pierce and Harry Carter, and that another man, Dr John Humbleby, will be the next victim. Unsure of how to respond, Luke feels that this is unimportant and pays lip service only.

However, he is soon surprised to find the obituaries of not only Miss Pinkerton, who has been killed in a hit-and-run car accident, but also a Dr Humbleby, who has died of septicaemia. Luke, a retired policeman, travels to this seemingly quiet village and poses as a researcher for witchcraft and superstition to try and uncover the true murderer. Staying in a large estate with the wealthy Gordon Whitfield and pretending to be a cousin of Bridget Conway (Whitfield's fiancee), he makes inquiries into the deaths. He and Conway receive the assistance of Honoria Waynflete, an elderly but observant spinster whom they believe may know the identity of the person behind the deaths. By asking several villagers — including Mr Abbot, a solicitor who fired Tommy Pierce from his service due to an incident with a letter; the Reverend Mr Wake, local preacher; Mr Ellsworthy, an antique shop owner who appears to be mentally insane, and Dr Thomas, Humbleby's medical partner (who had had several rows with Humbleby and would have benefited from his death) — it becomes apparent that the deaths had been understood to be accidents.

Amy Gibbs died after confusing her cough remedy with hat paint in the dark, Tommy Pierce died from falling off the library roof after cleaning the windows, Harry Carter fell from a bridge while drunk and drowned in the mud, and Humbleby died from a cut that became infected. Luke learns that Mrs Lydia Horton was another victim of these 'accidents' — she was recovering from acute gastritis and was progressively getting better before she had a sudden unexpected relapse and died.

Luke believes Ellsworthy to be the killer. He had shown signs of mental instability, and Luke's suspicions are further aroused after he sees Ellsworthy arriving home with blood on his hands, though this later is proved to be blood from a hen he sacrificed with his friends as part of a Pagan ritual. Later on in that day, Luke and Miss Waynflete witness Whitfield arguing with his chauffeur, Rivers, who had taken Whitfield's Rolls-Royce for a joyride. Shortly after this event, Rivers is found dead, with his skull caved in by a stone pineapple which Whitfield had outside his house for decoration.

Luke and Bridget have realised that they are in love with each other, and Bridget tells Gordon of her decision to break off the engagement. Gordon, ordering Luke to his study, makes a very suspicious statement. He claims, with some satisfaction, that God, executing divine justice upon wrongdoers, kills people that do him harm. Whitfield notes as examples that Mrs Horton had argued with him, Tommy Pierce did mocking impressions of him, Harry Carter shouted at him while drunk, Amy Gibbs was impertinent to him, Humbleby disagreed with him on the village water supply, and Rivers used his car without permission and then spoke disrespectfully to him; and all of them died soon afterwards. Whitfield predicts that Luke and Bridget, having wronged him, will soon meet their fates too.

This sudden turn of events makes Luke change his mind about who is responsible for the deaths. It seems obvious under the circumstances that Whitfield must be the murderer. He consults Miss Waynflete, who confirms his suspicions, and tells him of how she knew he was insane: when they were both young, Waynflete and Whitfield had been engaged to be married. But one evening, Whitfield killed one of her canaries that she kept as a pet, with the appearance that he enjoyed doing it. She knew from that moment on that Gordon went too far on subjects — so far that he would kill those who wronged him even slightly or trivially.

Luke and Bridget decide that Bridget should leave Whitfield's estate to stay at Miss Waynflete's house, to be protected from Gordon. Luke goes off to collect their luggage and prepare to leave, while Bridget and Honoria go for a walk in the woods. It is at this point that a sudden twist in the plot occurs: Honoria, of whom Bridget has had a nagging suspicion, reveals herself to be the murderer. During her engagement to Whitfield, Honoria had killed her own pet canary after it bit her, which prompted Gordon to abandon the engagement. She vowed revenge on Gordon, and eventually decided to have him hanged for crimes he did not commit. She came up with the plan to kill anyone with whom Gordon had any trouble, eventually leading his ego to become inflated with the idea (which she suggested to him) that God exacted immediate retribution from those who disrespected him.

Honoria regularly visited Lydia Horton, to whom Whitfield had sent some grapes, and was able to poison her tea. Honoria next killed Amy by swapping the bottles around in the night and locking the door from the outside using pincers. The fact that she died from hat paint would have suggested an old-fashioned touch, linking it in Luke's mind with an older man, like Gordon. She killed Carter by pushing him off the bridge on the day he had a row with Gordon, and she likewise pushed Tommy Pierce out of the window while he was working. Whitfield had been the one to assign this job to Tommy, so that made him look suspicious.

Lavinia Pinkerton had observed Honoria staring at Humbleby as he and Whitfield argued, and she realised that Honoria must be the killer, and that Humbleby would be her next victim. Suspecting that Lavinia had figured out the truth, Honoria followed Lavinia into London. Just after Lavinia and Luke had parted ways, Honoria pushed the other woman in front of a car that happened not to stop. Honoria framed Whitfield by giving a nearby witness the registration number of Whitfield's Rolls-Royce.

After inviting Humbleby round to her house, she was able to cut his hand with scissors, supposedly by accident. She then persuaded him to let her apply a dressing to the wound. She had previously infected the dressing with pus seeping from her cat's ear, and Humbleby died a few days later from blood infection. After witnessing Rivers being sacked, Honoria hit him with a sandbag and caved his skull in with the stone pineapple -- it would have appeared suspicious as it was a decoration that only Gordon chose. Finally, she drugged Bridget's tea (which, fortunately for Bridget, she had not actually drunk) and took her into the woods, where the two of them began talking.

Honoria then reveals a knife covered in Whitfield's fingerprints, and informs Bridget that she will kill her and leave the knife at the scene. Whitfield's fingerprints on the knife that killed the woman who had just jilted him would be damning evidence against him. Furthermore, Honoria had arranged for Whitfield to be seen walking alone through the very area where Bridget's body would be found. According to Honoria's plan, Whitfield would be condemned as a murderer and would surely be hanged. Bridget, who was about to have her throat slit, fights with the older woman, who has the wiry, mad strength of the truly insane. Having himself realised that Honoria was the killer, Luke arrives on the scene and saves Bridget. With the case over, Bridget and Luke decide to leave the village once and for all, to live their lives together as a married couple.

Once I've written a comprehensive summary like this, I check it contains everything that's in the overview. Once I'm satisfied, I put the overview away and concentrate on working from the summary. I will keep a copy of the premise (maybe attached to my cork-board) to make sure everything I write fits within it.

It's quite natural for the initial summary to contain blanks and unanswered questions. These can be filled in when you come to transfer the story into scenes and chapters, which is the next stage.

Think In Scenes

Novels, like movies and TV shows, are made up of scenes. I usually follow the James Patterson model and make each scene a short chapter by itself. Sometimes, I'll include two scenes in a single chapter, very occasionally three very brief ones, especially if I want to tinker with the pace. It all depends on how I feel and what I consider works best.

It's completely a matter of choice, provided you don't entirely disregard the conventions of your genre. You can have a dozen scenes in every chapter if that's what rocks your boat, provided your readers are prepared to accept it. This is something you need to find out when you do your initial research at Amazon.

Remember that a scene in a novel is not the same as a scene in a movie. Take a fight that starts in a bar and spills out into the street. In a movie, that'd take up at least two scenes (1. The Bar, interior; 2. The Street, exterior), in a novel, it's just one.

Think like a movie director. The biggest mistake beginners make is to think they have to show the action every step of the way. You don't. Two guys in a bar decide they're going to visit Big Mo. Next scene: they are shaking hands with Big Mo (or cracking his head open with a baseball bat). There's no need to see them get into the car, drive over, park, ring the bell, and so on...

Although it's generally a good rule to 'Show, don't tell,' sometimes it's better to summarise. Rather than write scenes where three cops knock on a dozen doors each in a 'door-to-door' canvassing session, you could tie it all up with a couple of lines of dialogue in the middle of an existing scene, like this:

'How did this morning's house-to-house go?' Lieutenant Jeeves asked Miller. 'Discover anything new?'

'Not a goddam thing, Lou. In that neighbourhood, they're all deaf, dumb, or blind.'

Building The Skeleton

THIS IS IT. Time to start outlining in earnest. To begin with, we're only thinking about scenes and not really worrying about chapters. That'll come later.

Using the summary as your guide, you need to write down a list of rough descriptions of the scenes you think you're going to need for the novel. At this stage, it's just a list. I don't add any detail unless I suddenly get an idea that's not in the summary, in which case I'll add it.

When you're thinking of scenes, there's no need to list them in order. Part of the list might look something like this:

- Don and Meg rob the convenience store.
- The final showdown with the FBI.
- Don shoots the Sheriff.
- Meg is captured by the FBI.
- Don rescues Meg.
- Doc Harper betrays Don and Meg.
- Meg's Trial, Day One.
- Don's mother's funeral.

If I'm working in Scrivener, these would be the names I'd

give the files in the binder. In a word processor, I'd make them headings.

The next step is to put the scenes in order. This is the part where you really should be working on having a complete story. Refer back to your summary and add to it and amend it as you feel fit. By the end of the process, you should have a summary that contains the main story of your novel or screenplay and a corresponding list of scenes.

Again, you don't have to worry too much if you don't think you've got the order exactly right. Sometimes, when I come to do the actual writing, ideas occur to me that sort out any chronological problems that might be niggling me.

Adding Sub-Plots

As we've already discussed, it's often a good idea to insert one or two sub-plots but only if they are in some way connected to the main story or serve some other purpose. A sub-plot cannot be contradictory to your premise. In fact, nothing in your novel can contradict the premise.

This is the time to work on sub-plots. They should be treated exactly like your main story. The only difference will be that they will be much shorter and subservient to the main plot. If they weren't, they wouldn't be sub-plots.

You simply need to write a summary of each sub-plot. My advice would be to not have more than two sub-plots in any novel or screenplay. Three separate stories in one novel — even if they are connected in some way — is enough for most readers of commercial fiction to have to cope with. Most authors will make do with one sub-plot; maybe even none.

Here's an example of a sub-plot Summary:

Fourteen-year-old Martha is texting a boy she met in an online chat-room. At least, she assumes he is a boy roughly her same age. Little does she know that CoolDude96 is actually a 46-year-old man who gets girls to send him naked selfies which he gets paid to upload to a subscription website frequented by paedophiles.

Martha has a row with her mother. Angry and upset, she is flattered by CoolDude96's attention. They have a flirty exchange of texts. Martha manages to resist the temptation to send him a naked selfie.

The next morning, Martha gets a text from CoolDude96, saying that he doesn't think she really is a fifteen-year-old (she lied about her age). Foolishly, Martha sends a selfie of her in school uniform standing outside the school gates. When she comes out of school, the 46-year old is waiting for her... (and so on...)

This type of sub-plot would work especially well if Martha's careerist mother was under pressure at work and not able to spend enough time with her daughter. Once the situation is revealed, it can add to mum's sense of guilt and make Martha feel even less loved.

A sub-plot can be useful for cranking up the pressure. Scenes can be alternated with the main plot to create extra tension for both plot strands. You now have to your sub-plot or sub-plots down into scenes and add them to the overall list of scenes in the most effective way possible. Don't worry about getting it exactly right. Until you publish your novel or screenplay, you have the power to change everything around, or leave it out entirely, if that's what you ultimately decide.

If you're anything like me, you'll keep seeing gaps where other scenes could go. I tend to quickly write these and put them into order. It's also important to delete any scenes that aren't working or which don't move the story forward in any real and meaningful way. Remember, you always have the option of deleting a scene and imparting the same information in other ways, such as have a character speak it in conversation.

Writing tutors always say, "Show don't tell," but they also say, "Don't bore your readers." That's *much* more important. If a 1,000-word scene is just plain boring, you'd be better off adding a line or two of dialogue somewhere else.

Don't be dismayed if you find you still have minor gaps in the plot. It's quite natural. Provided you know the main plot points, you'll be fine. As the wonderful Suspense novelist Patricia Highsmith wrote in her 1983 book, *Plotting & Writing Suspense Fiction*:

"I spoke earlier about the necessity of seeing a book as clearly as one sees a photograph, but I am almost never able to do this in the sense of seeing the whole *plot* as clearly as a photograph. I see my characters and the setting, the atmosphere, and what happens in the first third or quarter of a book, let's say, and usually the last quarter, but there is apt to be a foggy spot three-quarters of the way through, which I cannot clear up until I get there."

In our case, 'when we get there' is when we come to write the detailed chapter-by-chapter outline. I find that once I've worked out the journey up to that point, the gaps tend to fill themselves.

Putting Flesh On The Skeleton

IT'S time to turn the scenes into chapters. As I've already said, how many scenes per chapter is partly up to you and partly a case of following the conventions of your chosen genre or sub-genre.

You do need to consider *viewpoint*. In recent years it has become OK to tell a story through various different viewpoints throughout a novel. Again this is a matter of personal preference after you have checked on what other authors in your field are doing.

Just be careful you don't fall into any traps. For instance, if you're going to write only in the first person, you can't include information your character doesn't know. I personally prefer to use third person limited point of view, which doesn't hold me back as much. It also means I can follow whoever I want in a scene.

The final stage of the outlining process is to create summaries of a few hundred words per chapter. The summary should contain an overview of everything significant that happens. Try and plan every chapter so that it has a beginning, a middle, and an end. If possible, add a hook to the ending that will make the reader want to read the next chapter to find out more.

There is no hard and fast rule about creating chapters from scenes. My advice is not to think about it too much. Just get on and do it. You'll probably end up making changes before your start to write, anyway.

When you come to write each chapter summary, make a note of what you want to achieve within that chapter. What information do you want to give the reader? I find it helps to make a short list. The aim is to enable you to write the chapter of your novel using this summary alone.

Just start writing the chapter summaries. At this stage, I think it's unwise to add numbers to your chapter outlines. Save that for when you are confident you have everything in the right order. For me, that's usually when I've finished writing the novel! Until then you really need the freedom to swap stuff around. Maybe combine scenes into chapters or split them up. Just think how short and long chapters are going to affect the pace of your finished novel.

Here's an example of what I mean, taken from a non-existent novel that'll never get written:

Laney goes to see the old lady who witnessed the hit and run. Her name is Mrs Wilkinson; she is 84 years old and a widow. Her small, old-fashioned house smells of stale meat and lavender. The old lady insists on making tea for Laney and she serves it with homemade lemon drizzle cake. Laney finds the cake dry but tries not to show it. At first, Mrs Wilkinson says she didn't see anything, but Laney can tell she's lying.

Laney spots a photograph of a young man on her dresser and asks about him. It's her only son who was killed in Iraq. Laney talks about duty and tries to tease the information he needs out of her. Eventually, she admits that the man she saw driving the hit and run car looked like her neighbour, Mr Prentice, who frightens her. Laney says he'll make sure nothing happens to her, and takes his leave. Once the door has closed behind him, Mrs Wilkinson picks up her telephone and begins to dial a number…

I think it would be easy to take that summary and be able to quickly and easily write an 800-1,200 word chapter without much fuss. That's exactly why we're doing this. We are making the novel writing process as easy and blip-free as possible.

It's a good idea to write to outline as if you would for publication or for an agent or film producer to read. Make it as interesting as you can and you'll help yourself when you come to write the actual novel. You want to end up with an incredible sounding outline, one that contains references to smells, sounds, and emotions: anything that will help convey atmosphere and depth.

When you've written your chapter outline, put it to one side then come back a little while later and read it. Unless it's absolutely perfect, there are going to be areas you're not happy with. When I reread outlines that aren't quite 'ready', a little voice inside my head pipes up whenever I get to the parts that aren't right. This is the time to fix whatever's wrong.

Whenever I find myself running out of steam, I find it helps to remind myself what it is each of the characters involved in a scene hopes to gain. Are they being open about their motivation or are they trying to hide it? Who is allied with who? Usually these questions will help me untangle what needs saying.

A really good novel doesn't require much more effort than one that's mediocre or average. How good your novel or screenplay turns out to be will be related to how much effort you put into the outline. Without being too obsessive, try not be satisfied with second best.

Look at every chapter outline you've written for your novel and ask yourself: *What is it I'm trying to say?*

The next question should be: *How could it be improved?*

- Are there chapters that don't contribute anything to the story? *Get rid of them.*
- Is something missing? *Fix it.*
- Does what happens in a chapter look familiar? Might you have seen it in someone else's work? *Change it.*
- Are there any surprises in your story? Big surprises? *If not, create some.*
- Does your story plod along without much pace? *If so, tighten it up. Take out anything the reader will consider boring.*

If you have access to people who know about fiction, it might be an idea to let them take a look at your final outline. Be prepared for criticism, and take it on the chin. I strongly suggest you don't try and get opinions from anyone outside the world of writing or publishing. They simply will not have the relevant knowledge to help you and might very well make things worse.

The Finished Article?

WHEN YOU'VE GOT your outline just as good as you think you can get it, stop. What you have in front of you is essentially your novel in condensed form. All you have to do now is write the chapters.

You've already done more than half the work. Because you've put so much effort into the outline, the writing part will be much, much easier. *Trust me.*

By this stage, all your research should be done. Make sure it is. When you come to write, you do not want to have to keep stopping to check the name of the street that goes from Broadway to Wigmore Hill, or what the five-star hotel near the top of Mount Fuji is called.

All this information, together with character names and whatever, should already be in the outline waiting for you. Before I sit down to write any novel, I want to make sure everything is ready to go. I read over the outline one last time just to check I've not accidentally missed out anything. I'll show you what I mean...

This is a bad chapter outline:

Winston travels to see the man with the eye patch, He lives in a hotel. Winston finds him with a woman who attacks him. Winston wins and asks about the identity of the Blue Lotus. Rather than tell him, Dawson kills himself.

This is way better:

Winston takes the subway to the Excelsior Hotel on Broadway, where Dawson (the man with the eye patch) lives in the penthouse. The moment Winston emerges from the elevator, he is attacked by a black-clad female Chinese ninja-like bodyguard. She uses martial arts to attempt to disable Winston, but he is a black belt in karate and fights back. After a brief struggle, the ninja lunges at him with a short blade, which Winston manages to turn back on her and kill her. Dawson is shocked, and under pressure from a very angry Winston, agrees to fetch the information he wants. Although Winston tries to keep him close, Dawson manages to run through an open window and fall to his death, rather than reveal the truth about the Blue Lotus. Winston is back to square one.

Just think what would happen if you tried to write a chapter from the first synopsis. There's so much information missing, you'd be constantly checking facts, and looking things up. That's a huge waste of writing time.

Writing The Novel

How To Use The Outline

IF YOU'VE OUTLINED as I've suggested, you'll now be able to write your novel quickly and easily. Everything you need to write should be contained in those few pages of outline.

Pity other authors.

For them, the job of writing is the hardest bit. With my method, it becomes the easiest. Writing commercial fiction should not be a slow, agonising process. You get paid only for what you've written and so it helps if you can write as quickly and efficiently as possible.

This Is How You Do It...

Allow yourself at least one hour of uninterrupted writing time. In that hour you'll potentially be able to write as much as traditional writers used to manage in a day, provided you follow these very simple instructions. If you can't manage an hour, start with 15 or 30 minutes and work your way up.

You've got to concentrate. Improved concentration comes with practice. The more you can concentrate, the easier the writing process will be for you. There are online courses you can take to help you concentrate. Some of them are free to try out.

I've written a book called *1800 Words An Hour...* that goes into a lot more detail about writing quickly and efficiently. If you think you need help, search for it at your local Amazon store.

You need to write without distraction. I know it's not always easy, but you have to banish other members of your family from the writing room first of all. You cannot have people interrupting you, asking about clean shirts or 'What time's lunch?' when you're halfway through a chapter. Be firm but polite. If need be, leave the house altogether and go and write in a library or coffee shop.

What I call the 'writing room' is the room in which you are writing. It can be your kitchen at home, the library, your nearest Starbucks, a closet under the stairs, anywhere you are able to tap at a keyboard and write. When you start to earn millions from your novels, you'll be able to afford a special room just for writing. Until then, make do with what you've got.

Just make the writing room as quiet and free from distractions as you possibly can. Don't be obsessive or make a fuss about it. Almost everything you need to do can be achieved inside your own head.

Even a public room like the library or a coffee shop will have areas that are quieter and less likely to offer disturbances than others. These are the sections you should be seeking out, though you must avoid getting stressed if you can't get what you consider the ideal spot.

In this modern age, the internet offers huge distractions. During writing time, you should switch off your email and banish yourself from invidious distractions such as Twitter, Facebook, and Instagram. Don't think you can leave them running in the background: you can't.

When you've done all that, you are ready to start your

period of writing. When you find that an hour is not enough, you can make it two or more hours, if you want. The more I write, the easier it seems to become.

All writers have to make choices. I personally like to write my novels as quickly as I can to get them finished. My writing tends to take over my brain and I like to strike while the iron's hottest. I am self-employed so I have an advantage over most people, as I can write for as long as my brain will allow me.

Authors who have to juggle writing with family commitments, a full-time job, and maybe other distractions, have it hardest. But even they get to make choices.

What do you consider to be the best way to spend an hour, watching a rerun of House on the television, or writing a couple of chapters of your novel?

Would you rather have a night out with the boys (or girls) or finish some more chapters?

Which is more important to you, the football match or the novel?

I'll leave you to make your own conclusions. Obviously, everyone needs time off from writing, but a balance has to be struck.

Getting Started Writing

THE NATURE of this outlining process means you don't have to write the novel in any set order. The first chapter is usually the hardest to write, mainly because it is the first. You'll want to make sure it sparkles and that it's good enough to hook the reader, etc, etc.

To be fair, the first chapter really is the one that demands the most care and attention. The prospect of starting it can be daunting and has led to more writer's block than any other chapter.

To help me get started writing my new novel, I almost always ignore chapter one and pick a juicy chapter from the middle of the book. I look for one that involves plenty of action. Short, snappy paragraphs are good to warm up on.

Read the chapter outline carefully. Get a picture in your mind's eye of how the scene might play out. What would be its sounds and smells? Without being obsessive, it's often a great idea to add extra dimensions. As you're going in cold, you might want to read a couple of the preceding chapter outlines to get an idea of what's happening at that point in the novel.

Think of the best way to start the chapter. A line of

dialogue? Some kind of action? Try and avoid what's obvious. If characters are having a meeting, starting the chapter with their arrival at the venue is the safe but boring option. Maybe throw in an off-the-wall line such as: *Danny suspected he looked guilty before he'd even opened his mouth*. Only you will know how to do this.

Take a deep breath and start writing.

Write as fast as you can. Don't worry too much about wrong keys and spelling mistakes. Just get the words down as fast as possible.

Don't stop writing until you've finished the chapter. If you're like me, your chapters will be pretty short. Maybe 500-1,000 words. That shouldn't take long: half an hour maximum. Much less with practice.

When you've finished, feel very pleased with yourself. You've started writing your novel.

Now is the time to go back over what you've just written, correct the spelling and edit anything that doesn't work. After another few minutes, you'll be looking at a chapter that's good enough to be published.

Your choice now is to either carry on chronologically or else head back to the start. I usually go back and rush through chapter one, knowing full well I'll probably end up having to totally rewrite it before the novel is finished. But it doesn't matter. A chapter that's been written can be edited, a blank page is still a blank page.

Battling Writer's Block

Writer's Block comes in many shapes and sizes. Because we're working with such a detailed outline, the most common version — that of now knowing what to write — will be pretty much eliminated.

The version of writer's block that's most often fatal to beginners is the notion that what we are writing is no good.

Writers are funny. I'd be very surprised if someone who'd just decided to become a doctor thought they'd be able to perform a perfect heart transplant or oversee a ward full of patients on their first morning of training.

Similarly, anyone wanting to make jewellery wouldn't expect to come out of their initial class brandishing a Faberge-style egg they'd just knocked up. But for some reason, writers think their first novel should be the best ever written in the English language. If it's not, that must mean it's rubbish.

Wrong!

Don't stress on how great it is (or not), just get on with it. No matter how bad you think your writing is, I can guarantee there will be published examples that are much, much worse.

The important thing is to get the words down. Provided they make sense and move the story forward, they'll do. Authors of commercial fiction are storytellers. We are not trying to impress anyone with our purple prose. It may surprise you to know that readers definitely do not want purple prose. In fact, they will invariably run a mile to avoid it.

Look at the authors who sell the most books. People like James Patterson, Dan Brown, and Clive Cussler. I'll bet none of these guys would struggle for hours to find the perfect word that describes a butterfly's colouring. They'd just say, 'red butterfly' or 'scarlet butterfly,' if they mention the darn thing at all. You've got to be like that.

As a commercial novelist, your purpose is to write stories, to entertain. That's best achieved using clear, plain language.

It's *the cat sat on the mat*, NOT *the glorious feline ensconced itself on the delightful Persian weavings*.

When The Novel Is Written

PERSEVERE and you'll soon have your novel finished. How long it takes will depend on you, but I can guarantee it'll be many fewer hours than if you'd started writing without an outline.

When the novel is finally 'in the can', take a couple of days away from it. Then come back and read it all the way through, preferably in one sitting. If your outline worked, your novel should too. If you have any issues with pacing, you can edit and fine tune before you send it out to be professionally edited.

When you first started reading *Outline Your Books Or Die!*, I'll bet you found it daunting. But now that you've written a novel using my outlining system, you'll know it's really quite easy. The crucial thing is not to let all the words overwhelm you.

There is no right way and no wrong way to write a novel. As far as I can see, there are only degrees of difficulty. Of course, the quality of the end result is also variable. If you can read and write and if you've followed my advice closely, you should have no problem regarding quality. You may not have written the best novel of all time, but I can guarantee it'll be far better than the majority of what's available on Kindle now.

About the Author

A Note From The Author

Thanks for staying with me right to the end. I'll bet outlining a novel isn't as difficult as you thought it was and I wish you every success with your writing.

Please review this book

Leaving a review on Amazon, Barnes & Noble, or wherever you bought this book, whether good or bad, helps others find the best products. I'd appreciate it if you could please find the time to write one.

To check out other books on writing, please visit my AllFictionWriting.com website and visit the 'Books For Writers' page.

At the same time, you could also sign up to my email list to receive free occasional emails containing up to date writing tips and important news for writers. I hate spam as much as you do, so I won't be sharing your email address with anybody, I promise.

Get the next book for free!

Click here to get started: www.AllFictionWriting.com

Thanks again for reading.

All the best,

The Writers' VIP Club

Sign up to my email list to receive free emails containing up-to-date writing tips and important news for writers.

I hate spam as much as you do, so I won't be sharing your email address with anybody, I promise.

Click here to join Jim Driver's Writers' VIP Club and get your next book for free!

FREE DOWNLOAD!

Sign up to my Writers' VIP Club email list and get another of my popular 'How to Write' books for FREE!

Please Review This Book!

Thank you for staying with me to the end. I hope you've learned lots and that I've helped you write faster and more clearly.

If you have any questions regarding this book or about writing in general, please email me. My private address is jim@allfictionwriting.com.

Please review this book. Whether good or bad, a review helps others find the best products.

All the best,

Click here to review on Amazon

About the Author

Jim Driver was born in Yorkshire, in the north of England, in 1954. After being kicked out of college for not studying law properly, he became an event and festival organiser, before finally settling down as a writer, editor, and publisher.

Jim wrote about music, beer and food for *Time Out* magazine in London for almost 20 years and founded acclaimed independent publishing house, The Do-Not Press, in the heady 1990s. He has ghost-written several novels and published even more under various names.

Jim now lives beside the seaside in Ramsgate, East Kent, and is currently working on a series of mystery novels.

More Books by Jim Driver

How To Write A Novel The Easy Way: Using the Pulp Fiction Method to Write Better Novels

Want to write a novel?

What's holding you back? *Lack of confidence? Not sure where to start?*

There has never been a better time to be a writer, provided you know how best to go about it.

In this short but to-the-point introduction to writing fiction, publisher, editor and author, Jim Driver reveals the secrets the experts use to write bestselling novels.

Taking inspiration from the classic Pulp Fiction writers of the golden era, Jim shows how to banish writers' block forever and reveals the easiest ways you can create and plot commercial novels.

Don't let your doubts hold you back. Let Jim show you how you can take action and start writing your profitable novel series today.

New edition.

Reviews of Previous Editions:

"Right to the point, no fluff or filler, just what I was looking for as a starter guide to writing. Will definitely read Jim's other books in the future." *Amazon Customer, Amazon.com.*

"I loved this book, I really did. I found it refreshing, full of no-nonsense honest advice that tells it like it is, a book in which the author likens the old pulp fiction books to modern Kindle short novels." *Poet's Wife, Amazon.co.uk*

It's time to start your novel. *Download your copy of* How To Write A Novel The Easy Way *today.*

~

How To Write The Million Dollar Story

What separates great novels and blockbuster movies from the thousands of others?

Just one thing: STORY.

Once you know the secrets of crafting great stories, you've got it made...

Writing a great story should be the aim of every author. Once you've utilised the story-telling secrets contained in *Million Dollar Story*, you'll be able to repeat it over and over again – just like other super-successful storytellers, such as J.K. Rowling, Dan Brown, George R. R. Martin, Gillian Flynn, James Patterson, and Stephen King.

Readers, publishers, and studio heads don't care how accomplished a writer you are. The only question they want answered is, *"How good is the story?"*

When a novel is made into a movie or TV adaptation, the studios aren't paying for great prose, dazzling dialogue, or scintillating syntax – they ONLY WANT THE STORY.

New edition.

Filled with story examples from blockbuster novels, movies and TV, comprehensive checklists, and practical hands-on help, *How To Write The Million Dollar Story* gives you all the skills you need to make you an expert storyteller.

Don't waste any more of your valuable time, grab your copy today.

∾

Outline Your Books Or Die!

Why you definitely should outline your novel or screenplay

Spoiler Alert: this book may change the way you write forever…

It's not enough just to know how to outline, you have to know how to create a commercially successful story in the shortest possible time. Even 'pantsers' are working with outlines: it's why they write a first draft, second draft and so on…

Don't waste any more of your valuable writing time producing draft after draft: learn how to outline properly and efficiently.

Author, publisher and editor Jim Driver spent months taking seminars with famous authors and gurus like Robert McKee and James Patterson. He's read practically every book on novel planning, outlining, and plotting ever written (slight exaggeration) and worked on quite a few novels and screenplays himself.

Armed with all the information he collated over years, Jim has worked out a simple new way of outlining that makes the process of story writing far simpler than you'd expect and practically foolproof.

This new method of outlining works in every genre and will help you outline and write a commercially successful novel or screenplay in less time than you ever thought possible. Story engineering has never been so simple.

Don't settle for just writing a novel or screenplay. Discover how to outline properly and aspire to write the best commercial fiction you can.

New edition.

Reviews of Previous Editions:

"What I really loved about this book is that it's not scary. Jim Driver has broken the process down so well and he takes us by the hand so gently that we've taken one little step, and then another little step, and then one more step and suddenly we've walked across the rickety rope bridge and crossed the scary chasm without even noticing all the terrifying steps along the way and we are over the other side wondering how we got here with our finished novel clasped tightly in our hot little hands." *Diane W, Amazon.com*

"As a pantser trying to become a plotter, I've read lots of writing guides. This is by far the best and most useful I've found." *John B, Amazon.co.uk*

Can you afford to leave it to chance? Grab your copy of this short but invaluable book today.

∼

How To Write Dialogue That Sparkles

Better dialogue writing for novels, plays and screenplay writing

Dialogue must never be dull, or else your novel or screenplay will fail.

Is your dialogue holding you back?

As you know, every bestselling novel or blockbuster screenplay has a great story. The other most important aspect is dazzling dialogue.

Let editor, author, publisher and critic, Jim Driver show you how writing great dialogue can be fun and simple.

Among the topics covered in this concise 25,000 word book:

- Why dialogue is so important

- What dialogue is, and what it shouldn't be

- Four tricks to let your reader know who's speaking…

- The correct ways to format dialogue (and some interesting ideas you might not have heard of)

- 8 tricks to make your dialogue instantly more appealing

- How to tell a story through what people say to each other

- How to make each and every character sound individual and interesting

- Ten tips that will always improve your dialogue

Don't struggle with dialogue any longer. You'll find all the answers you need in this entertaining and concise book. Illustrated with examples from hit screenplays and novels, ranging from Graham Greene, F. Scott Fitzgerald and P.G. Wodehouse via pulp fiction classics, to modern icons such as *Breaking Bad*, J.K. Rowling, and James Patterson.

New edition.

Reviews of Previous Editions:

"This is a great how to on dialogue. This author clearly knows his stuff. I'm writing a book for kindle as a first time author and this book was very helpful." *JJ, Amazon.com*

"I learnt loads from this book. I'm glad that many points and improvements were what I'd been doing already, but there's never any harm in learning more. Definitely recommending this to others!" *Amazon Customer, Amazon.co.uk*

What are you waiting for? Make the move to drastically improve your dialogue writing skills today.

∼

1800 Words An Hour

Want to double your word count & writing quality?

Now you can. It's easy, thanks to my QC (Quicker and Clearer) Writing System.

I learnt how to write quickly the hard way.

To pay off mounting debts, I agreed to ghost-write a series of novels. Problem was, I'd written a number of non-fiction books, but I'd never finished a novel in my life!

My word count was pathetic: less than 5,000 words a week.

I had no other options. I wasn't looking forward to the HARD SLOG of writing and I had no idea what I'd do about WRITER'S BLOCK. In the end, I found a brilliant way of increasing my word count and making the writing ENJOYABLE.

And everyone said the books I'd ghostwritten were great!

I had stumbled on a wonderful way to increase my word count *and* write better books. I worked on it, improved the techniques by trial and error and I doubled my word count again!

Now I can't wait to get out of bed in the mornings and start writing!

In my short eBook (13,000 words) I'll show you how to write fast, clear, readable text all day, every day. Whether you're writing novels or non-fiction my QC (Quicker and Clearer) Method will help YOU write much more than 1800 words an hour.

In fact, my average word count has rocketed to between 2,000 and 2,500 words of USEABLE text every hour I sit down to write. This means I can write a complete novel every few weeks.

Want to know more?

My QC (Quicker & Clearer) System changed my life for the better.

Are you going to see how you can reach word counts of 2k up to 10k?

New edition.

Reviews of Previous Editions:

"Need to boost your word productivity and speed, this is the book that will show you how." *Melissa Sugar-Gold (reviewing* 1,600 Words an Hour*), Amazon.com*

"The tips and tricks go farther than practice (however daily writing is a big part of speed). I'd figured out most of it on my own but the two or three new techniques I learned made the book more than worth the investment." Glenn Hawkins *(reviewing* 1,600 Words an Hour*), Amazon.com*

Why delay? Speed up your writing speed and improve your productivity today.

∿

The Twenty 20 Worst Fiction Writing Mistakes That Can Destroy Your Novel Writing Career

What simple mistakes could you be making that are cheating you of success?

Advice to writers usually consists of 'rules' and 'tips' which are either too broad to be helpful or else just plain wrong. Maybe the problem is more straightforward than you are thinking?

This concise instructional manual shines a spotlight on what new writers cannot know, including the answers to these questions:

- How do I get started as a successful writer?

- What simple tricks can I employ to make my dialogue 100% better?

- What type of books should I be writing?

- Is there a quick and easy way to outline?

- How do I find out what readers want?

- Why does my fiction not sell?

- What is the single biggest secret that can massively improve my sales?

• and much more…

Jim Driver has been a writer, editor and publisher for almost forty years. He admits he's made all the mistakes in the book, but he has learned from them! This 20,000 word ebook is guaranteed to improve any author's chance of success.

New edition.

Reviews of Previous Editions:

"I enjoy the Jim Driver books. He delivers what the cover promises in the most simple and straight forward way. Always worth the 60 minute investment to see the down and dirty truths of writing." *Zen Dragon, Amazon.com*

"Mr. Driver offers lots of no-nonsense advice for aspiring writers like me. I'm happy to report that I haven't made all 20 mistakes myself, but I've made my share.." *Steve Merryman, Amazon.com*

Find out how you can prevent yourself from falling into writing traps before you waste any more of your valuable time.

Outline Your Books Or Die!

Secrets of Writing Fiction that Sells, Plotting, Novel Outlining Techniques
by
Jim Driver
www.AllFictionWriting.com

Version 3.0
April, 2020
Includes major rewriting and new bonus chapters

Printed in Great Britain
by Amazon